HIST

306.81 D265L
Davitz, Lois Jean.
Living in sync
$18.95

DISCARD

Memphis and Shelby
County Public Library and
Information Center

MAIN LIBRARY

For the Residents
of
Memphis and Shelby County

Other Books By The Authors

Making It from 40–50

How to Live Almost Happily with a Teenager

Language of Emotion

Communication of Emotional Meaning

Love and Understanding

The Psychiatric Patient: Case Histories

Evaluating Research Proposals in the Behavioral Sciences: A Guide

Living in Sync:
Men and Women in Love

Living in Sync: Men and Women in Love

Lois Leiderman Davitz, Ph.D.
Joel Robert Davitz, Ph.D.

The Bergh Publishing Group, Inc.

New York

Copyright © 1986 by Lois and Joel Davitz
All rights reserved.
No part of this book may be reproduced or used in any form without written permission from the publisher except in the case of reviews.
Published in the United States of America in 1986 by The Bergh Publishing Group, Inc., c/o E. P. Dutton, Inc., 2 Park Avenue, New York, N.Y. 10016
Portions from sharing fun and pleasure appeared originally in *McCall's* magazine.

Printed in the United States of America

ISBN 0-930267-22-2

*Living in Sync
Men and Women
in Love Not for Just the
Moment
Not for a Couple of Years
But for a Lifetime*

Acknowledgments

The thoughts and feelings of many men and women between the ages of 20 and 50 plus are reflected in this book. We would like to express our deepest appreciation, respect, and gratitude for their time, interest, and cooperation.

L. L. D.
J. R. D.

Contents

Living in Sync	*13*
The Twenties Establishing Identities	*25*
The Thirties The Status Decade	*59*
The Forties The Age of Reassurance	*85*
The Fifties Plus Reconciliation	*107*
Making It Work	*117*
Sharing Fun and Pleasure	*133*
Evaluating the Sync of Your Relationship	*145*
Sync Assessment Test	*147*
Scoring the Test	*155*
Interpreting Your Test Results	*158*

Living in Sync

Living in sync. What a marvelous description of marriage as it *should* be! Two people living together in perfect rhythm and harmony, each moving in balance with the other, so that the sum of their lives is greater than each life lived independently. A man and woman creating an enduring, intimate relationship that becomes the central core of meaning in their lives—that's what marriage should be all about.

Cynics of this generation might dismiss such notions as romantic fantasies of a past age. In the twentieth century marriages often run the risk of being more like business operations with checks and balances, debits and credits. But is this what you really want? Is this what any man or woman desires?

AN IDEAL MATE

An ideal spouse. Isn't that what men and women fantasize about? After all, if you're going to spend night after night sleeping with someone and seeing that same person day after day, it makes good sense that you would want to do this with an ideal person.

There's nothing wrong with having fantasies about an ideal spouse. Thinking about marrying a dream man or a dream woman is a very normal thing to do. However, what people often don't realize is that our perceptions of an ideal spouse change over time, and that this change can affect a marriage by throwing the delicate balance of the relationship out of sync.

Phyllis, 38 years old, told us: "I had no idea how changed my husband had become. It seemed that one day I woke up, and there was a stranger in bed with me—a stranger who moved out of the house that afternoon, leaving his clothes behind in a closet."

"You're the same woman I married fifteen years ago," Greg told Phyllis just before he left.

"What's wrong with that?" Phyllis remembers saying. "It was fine for you then."

"But not now," he answered.

Only in Greg's opinion had Phyllis lost sparkle, verve, charm, "fizz." He still respects her as a person: "She's got a lot to offer. I don't deny that. It's just that my idea of what I want in a wife has changed."

Phyllis is trying to piece together the events that led to the break-up of the marriage: "Sure we had problems. Doesn't everybody? But we didn't have more than other people do."

Greg's clothes hang in the closet. Small possessions of his—a sailboat collection, assorted stamp albums—still sit on bookshelves. "It's my way of thinking he's going to come back," Phyllis explains.

At first there were tears. Tears gave way to anger. Anger

gave way to numbness. Numbness gave way to trying to sort the past into a meaningful pattern. The nagging question that haunts Phyllis is how Greg's notion of an ideal wife could possibly have changed.

"He pursued me. I never chased him," said Phyllis, recalling their premarriage dating. "He would race up the steps to my house. I can still picture him—so boyish-looking." She remembers how he would run his hands through her hair as they walked in the park. She recalls his "hanging" on her every word, watching her, reacting with affection every time she made a move. The look in his eye and the tone of his voice showed Phyllis that she was his dream girl.

Greg would not deny this fact. He recalls his stunned feelings when he, an "ordinary" guy, lucked out and captured the attentions of Phyllis, whom he described as a "terrific-looking female with a gorgeous body and a million-dollar smile."

Going to the beach with her on a hot summer afternoon was both pleasure and torture for Greg. There was pleasure in the way other guys noticed Phyllis and torture in the pleasure-pain of his unfulfilled desire for sex.

And how about Phyllis? How did Greg strike her when she was 22? "Passion—yes. But no way was I going to rush into sex with him until I was sure of how I felt. My friends envied me. Greg didn't have any idea how good-looking he was. That was part of what was so precious about him. He had that little-boy charm. It's no wonder I fell in love. He didn't even know girls were swooning all over him."

Their respective families saw the marriage as a storybook wedding of two young and handsome people who wore the charm of youth and the magic of romantic love like a halo around their heads. "Two children, one house, one dog, and four fish later, we are strangers to each other—a storybook with a bad ending, that's for sure," says Phyllis after the divorce.

Was it the hassles with the kids that split them?

Was it the series of disasters that hit that one miserable winter that marked the beginning of the end?

Was it the weariness that came from juggling a job, the children, and the house and left her too tired to want sex some nights that caused the break-up? Or was it her irritation with his all-consuming interest in his job that did it?

Contrary to what either of them think, it wasn't a specific incident or even a series of incidents that forced Greg to change his mind about the idyllic quality of their marriage. Sure, there were low periods. But there were also plenty of highs. In fact, when Greg finally faced the situation, he realized it wasn't Phyllis who had changed, nor the kids, nor the world around him. The changes in his desires and his notions of an ideal wife came from within himself.

What happened to Phyllis and Greg isn't all that unusual. Every couple knows that at some time or other during the course of a marriage or a relationship one of the pair will come up with a critical comment such as, "You're not what I want in a wife/husband. I married one person and now I find myself with someone completely different." Much of the basis for marital dissatisfaction comes when one or the other spouse no longer fits an ideal image.

Years ago, if we had heard about the break-up of Phyllis and Greg's marriage, some of us would have shaken our heads in disgust at Greg's immaturity. What kind of lame excuse is it to break up a lovely home because suddenly the man thinks his wife lacks zest? Greg's behavior would have astonished friends and family. Indeed, every time a so-called idyllic relationship ended, people were stunned.

Furthermore, having a fixed or stable attitude toward oneself and one's life used to be equated with being a mature person. Individuals who changed in any major way were more often than not put down as being childish and immature. A mature person simply didn't walk out on a spouse and children, divorcing himself from all the routines of his life overnight.

IDEALS CHANGE

It was just assumed that the person Greg thought of as an ideal spouse in his early twenties, for example, would also continue to be the love of his forties. And it would have been expected that, once Phyllis made up her mind about a man in her twenties, she would continue to find him her dream man a few decades down the road.

However, we now know differently. In the past decade or so a series of psychological studies has drastically altered the way we look at adulthood. There has been a growing awareness that men and women change as they grow older.

Thus, when Greg walked out of his house with only a small suitcase, bought himself a wardrobe of jeans, fancy sports jackets, and a gold chain for his neck, thought about opening up a coffee house, and considered having an adventure with a woman who was far more spirited than Phyllis, we cannot jump to the conclusion that he had "gone off the deep end."

Phyllis says that Greg has "lost his sanity." She insists that his behavior is abnormal. What she fails to realize is that, when we consider the developmental stages and characteristics of adult males over the years, what happened to Greg was predictable! The dream girl of his youth had lost the sparkle of attraction for him in his middle years. He's not the same man in his desires and, contrary to what Phyllis may believe, she is not the same woman.

Fifteen years ago Phyllis's notion of an ideal mate was a man who liked good wines, fun trips, candlelit restaurants. Greg met this need and she married him, delighted she had found an ideal. Now, more than a man with a knowledge of wines, Phyllis needs a man who remembers to take the kids to the orthodontist and pick up his own shirts from the laundry since she has a full-time job.

Although you may be convinced that your fantasy of an ideal spouse is going to remain the same forever, this simply isn't true. Certainly some values will endure. But as we grow older, the reality of life is that we change, and these changes proceed in predictable ways. Our belief is that, couples who know what men and women typically want in a spouse at certain given ages can be spared some of the emotional trauma that inevitably accompanies change.

IMPLICATIONS OF CHANGE

Marriage is not two people fixated in a static mold year after year. In fact, it involves two people who are both developing and changing throughout their lives. And, as a result, the marital relationship must change and develop throughout a marriage.

When two people assume that they have "established" a marital relationship, and that this relationship will remain stable and unvarying, they are bound to run into troubles. Because both of them are changing in the normal course

Living in Sync

of human development, *their relationship must also change to reflect their own patterns of development.* If they try to force their changing psychological needs into a static mold of marriage, they will only experience mutual frustration and unhappiness.

DEVELOPING IN SYNC

With both husband and wife in a process of continuing change and development, there are bound to be times when their patterns of development are out of sync. Each of us develops at his or her own rate, and each of us has a unique pattern and style of development. As a result, even in the happiest of marriages, there will be periods in which the changing interests, concerns, and needs of one person don't fit in with those of the other. These are the normal bumpy periods of every marriage.

But these normal developmental problems can be further complicated by a lack of understanding and misinterpretation of what is happening. When this occurs, marital difficulties arise, not only because husband and wife have different central needs at the time, but also because they are likely to misinterpret each other's behavior. When a wife sees her 45-year-old husband straining at the leash of everyday family responsibilities and hears him talk about escaping to some far-off desert island, she may misinterpret his behavior as evidence that he doesn't love her anymore. On the basis of this misinterpretation, she may well react with greater demands for attention and further proof of his continuing devotion. And, before they are aware of what's happening, they find themselves caught in a vicious circle of marital battles that can only hurt both of them.

UNDERSTANDING THE NORMAL COURSE OF DEVELOPMENT

To deal with these kinds of problems rationally and effectively, and to establish the necessary foundation for living in sync, we must understand the normal pattern of changing adult needs within the context of the marital relationship. It's not enough simply to recognize the fact that adults develop and change; we must understand an individual's development in relation to his or her marriage. Specifically, we must understand how the normal changes a person goes through in life influence and affect that person's relationship with his or her spouse. It is only on the basis of that kind of understanding that we can hope to achieve marriage in sync.

IDEALS REFLECT NEEDS

Asked to describe an Ideal Mate, a person's response certainly reflects his or her current concerns, needs, and interests relevant to marriage. For example, suppose a woman is concerned about her economic security and needs a husband who can assure her of that security. When asked to describe an ideal mate, her response will surely include some reference to a husband's financial status or capacity to earn money. Similarly, a man primarily concerned with advancing in his career will describe an ideal wife in terms that reflect his needs and interests. Thus, by studying people's descriptions of their Ideal Mates, we can gain insight into their needs and concerns as related to marriage. And, by studying people at different ages, we can obtain a picture of how these needs change and develop throughout the adult years.

Living in Sync

left out valuable elderly

Our study included 400 men and 400 women, married, divorced, and single between the ages of 20 to slightly over 50. These individuals all responded to questionnaires and a randomly selected sample from the various age groups participated in in-depth interviews. The individuals in the study came from all walks of life and lived in various parts of the United States.

We've changed the participants' names and altered identifying characteristics of specific people whenever necessary to protect the anonymity of those who were involved in the research. Nevertheless, as you read you're bound to pause and say to yourself: "I know someone exactly like that person." Or, you might say to yourself: "That's what happened to me." What is far more important, however, is not the identification you might feel but the understanding you will gain about how marriage-related needs and interests change and develop during adulthood.

UNDERSTANDING IS A FIRST STEP

Love is not enough. Good intentions are not enough. And, as experience has shown so often in the divorce courts, mechanically following the outward conventions of marriage is not enough.

There's no simple, magic formula for a marriage in sync. Let's be clear about that right at the outset. Life, and especially married life, is much too complicated to be lived successfully and meaningfully by following a simple formula.

Agree

It takes human understanding to live in sync and there's no substitute for it. Without mutual understanding, love is bound to die as husband and wife face the inevitable problems of living and growing together.

Of course, understanding alone doesn't guarantee living in sync. But it's a first step, a necessary first step in establishing a relationship in sync.

UNDERSTANDING WHAT?

Mutual understanding doesn't involve any high-flown, technical knowledge dressed up in long, fancy words. But that doesn't mean it's simple and easy and uncomplicated either. After all, we're dealing with human lives, and there are few really meaningful things in life that are simple, easy, and uncomplicated.

What is necessary is to understand some fundamental ideas about human life and become aware of some basic principles of living. In our forty plus years of married life and in our professional lives, we've learned a great deal. And it's this learning that we want to share to help you take an active stance in your own life, to achieve happiness in your marriage not just for the moment, not for a couple of years, but for a lifetime.

THE TWENTIES

Establishing Identities

What are little girls made of? Sugar and spice and everything nice—and for men in their twenties, mostly sex.

Leo, a nice-looking guy currently employed in an advertising agency, is 24 years of age. He has a number of career plans in mind. When he has had more business experience, he intends to open up his own firm. A sports enthusiast, a dedicated "health nut," he spends many free hours at a health club working out on the machines or doing laps in the pool with a fierce dedication.

Leo doesn't like people who smoke or drink. An environmentalist, he believes smoking pollutes the air. This represents a new attitude for Leo; he recently quit smoking himself. But his mission against smoking reflects his general exuberance and positive approach to life. Friends find his infectious sense of humor and kind, considerate manner completely irresistible.

Women who work in the office enjoy his company. One co-worker commented: "I don't have to worry about Leo's hands when I bend over for a drink at the water fountain." Another noted that she wouldn't panic if she found herself alone with him in a stalled elevator. Many of his female colleagues admitted they would enjoy dating him. Cindy, for example, who made the comment about the elevator, described him as shy, sweet, a lovely conversationalist, someone who really seems to have an interest in what his women co-workers are doing and thinking.

But what does Leo think about women? What does he want most from a date? What is his ideal? Sex.

When Leo thinks about a woman, he thinks about sex in the morning, sex at noon, and sex again at night before falling asleep. "And I wouldn't mind if she got me up in the middle of the night for a little bit more."

His idea of a perfect date with a woman isn't going to the museum all day, as some girls like Cindy think, but spending the day in bed with a terrific body and a face to match.

"Every look of this fantasy woman should spell sex appeal. Of course," he added, "I'd also like this bombshell of a sex-object to have brains." But, for Leo, brains alone don't count for much in a relationship unless the brains are "packaged right."

In response to the question "What is the first thing you think about when you meet a woman for the first time?" Leo unhesitatingly responded: "How she'll be in bed!"

Leo is not unique. He's not over-sexed. He's not a male chauvinist. Leo is typical of the vast majority of men in their twenties.

With very few exceptions, young males in this age group fantasize about an ideal woman in physical terms. Certainly other traits are considered, and we'll turn to those later.

But, first and foremost, the twenties decade of males finds sex pretty much synonymous with the word *ideal.*

In the open-ended interviews and on the questionnaires they completed, the men were free to describe an ideal woman in any way they wished. In one way or another sex invariably headed the list of topics discussed. Sex appeal was the overwhelming choice of the great majority of men in their twenties as a number-one trait in an ideal woman.

Sex appeal and physical attractiveness is uppermost in these men's minds even in the most casual contact with the opposite sex. It should be kept clearly in mind that what constitutes sex appeal and beauty differs markedly among men in their twenties. We showed a group of them pictures of women, also in their early twenties, and asked the men to select the photo of the one who most closely approximated their ideal of physical beauty and sexiness. It was evident from the wide range of choices that being sexy and attractive in one man's eyes didn't mean the same woman would also be sexy in another's.

IS THERE MORE THAN SEX?

"This doesn't mean there shouldn't be other things to a relationship," commented Mark, 25 years old, "but without the sexual part—how a woman behaves in bed—you might as well forget a relationship."

A friendly young man with an M.B.A. degree, Mark likes women, enjoys their company and dating. Serious about a career, he has no trouble respecting women's goals and talents career-wise. "It's great that women work, have equality. It'll make my life easier when I get married. I won't have to bring in all the income to support a family."

Although Mark wants a prospective spouse to work, he also wants to be sure that besides a job and doing all the other things in life, she doesn't get overworked and become too tired to be a delicious bed-partner.

WHAT DRIVES THE TWENTIES MALES?

Arlene, 26, a manager with a large insurance company, feels that men today have a perverted attitude toward women: "I am *not* a one-dimensional creature only designed for sex." Like many young women, Arlene can't understand why the dramatic changes of the past several decades haven't convinced men that women aren't sexual objects or toys: "Can't men finally get it into their heads that women are equal to men in every aspect of life?"

In order to understand the way men think, we must first separate these males' attitudes toward women as a group and their beliefs about an ideal woman. In their minds, there is a big difference between women in general and a woman in their fantasy life.

Richard, 24 years old, has no problem working with women: "My boss is a woman. She's a great person. Between you and me, I prefer a woman as a boss. When I tell her I want a day off, I don't get any flack. She understands. I've learned a helluva lot from her. She didn't get to be a vice president for nothing. For me, it's like having a private professor in management skills. Only studying with her is not a make-believe school. Everything that goes on is for real."

Richard's boss is about ten years older than Richard. They work long hours together and frequently meet for lunch. "Not once," said Richard, "has a sexual thought crossed my mind. She's nice-looking. Attractive. I'm just not interested in that kind of relationship with her."

Richard is not a male chauvinist. He respects the woman's professional skills. But, when he thinks about someone he would like to date, someone with whom he would like to spend his after-work hours, his thinking undergoes dramatic changes. The last thing he wants then are managerial skills, or the ability to read computer printouts. What does Richard think about?

"It's not that I have to jump into bed with a woman on a first date, though that's not a bad idea when you come to think about it. But I like a woman who appeals to me physically. If I date her a second time, and I continue to date her, there has to be the possibility that we're going to make it sexually. If I get the idea there's no chance or she's going to hold me off and play games, you won't find me wasting my time. I'll look elsewhere."

A sexually-satisfied man in his twenties walks a little taller, shoulders back a little more, chin up just a fraction. There's an undeniable air of masculine confidence enveloping him, an invisible but nonetheless discernible mantle, that certainly wouldn't be there if his performance in bed left something to be desired.

SEX AND MALE IDENTITY

Of course, men of all ages have sexual drives; however, for men in their twenties, the fact that they think, talk, dream, and fantasize about sex has a lot to do with their identity as males. Every stage in life is characterized by central issues and concerns. In the twenties, the major issue is one of identity. At some point both males and females in this age group have to confront the question, "Who Am I?"

Psychologists once thought that the question "Who Am I?" was resolved in adolescence. However, in the last few years, more and more observers of human behavior and adult development have become aware that this is not the case. "Who Am I?" continues to be a concern throughout the twenties and often recurs later in a person's life in one form or another.

One of the major questions males and females have to answer for themselves regarding "Who Am I?" involves sexual identity. With men, in particular, the sexual drive begins to peak in their twenties. Physically and psychologically, the twenties have been described as a period when a male's sexual interests and concerns about his sexual prowess and potency reach a peak.

As boys move from childhood to adulthood they begin to find out who they are as males. Fathers, mothers, sisters, girl friends, boys in the locker room—all provide tidbits of instruction. However, it's usually not until late adolescence that most males begin to have opportunities to answer the question for themselves, to confirm to themselves and to the outside world that they're potent, powerful males, able to make it in bed with the opposite sex.

It's tremendously important that men get a chance to proclaim their masculinity. Thus, a man in his twenties struts, flexes his muscles, and shows in many different ways appropriate to his personality, social background, or vocation that he is sexually powerful and potent.

Men have a need to communicate the message to themselves, to women, to other men: "Look at me. I'm a potent and powerful male."

"I FELT LIKE THROWING A GLASS OF WATER AT HIM"

And how do women in their twenties feel about the males' concern with sex? Disbelieving. Annoyed. Irritated. Uncomfortable. Resentful. Not one young woman in our study said, "Great. I like being a sex object. I like knowing the first thing men look at is the size of my breasts."

Rather, the vast majority agreed with Margaret, 24, who told us, "I resent the idea that I'm a sex object. Of course I want guys to notice me. Sure, I feel flattered when someone tells me I have a great figure. I'm human. It's normal for women to want to be seen as physically attractive by men. But it bothers me that so many guys seem to have one thought on their minds. That's what gripes me. Like last week I met this guy in law school. I'm a paralegal, and I'm thinking about law school.

"I thought to myself, 'How terrific. Here's someone with whom I have lots in common.' We would have a lot to talk about. We went out to dinner. It crossed my mind that I really hoped we would get to know one another better.

"We were talking. I was telling him about the firm where I worked. I asked him about law school. He had had a couple of drinks and he was smiling, listening, and then he leaned across the table and said, 'You've got a terrific body.' He told me that was the first thing he noticed when we met. I felt like throwing a glass of water at him. He wasn't drunk. He was dead serious.

"I thought, 'How crude.' He knew I felt embarrassed and yet he made it worse by continuing to joke. I sat through that dinner feeling awful, degraded, and humiliated. I felt like I was being made a fool of. The worst

part was at the beginning of the evening I thought he was someone I could really go for."

It bothers Margaret and many women that sex is so much on men's minds that they have trouble going through the pretenses of getting to know someone on a first date: "All men think about is how quickly they can jump into bed. They don't want to waste time on small talk."

"I hate the game of cat and mouse," said Lynn. "Some of the guys I date hardly give me a chance before they're trying to crawl all over me. I asked this guy once, 'Don't you want to know more about me? Wouldn't you like to know what I do?' And his answer was, 'I want to have fun with you, not talk about your job.'"

In the last several decades there has been a remarkable loosening up of sexual inhibitions and standards of male and female behavior. However, despite the changes in women's overt behavior, when women in their twenties describe an ideal man, they talk about a relationship, not sex. If anything, these women are opposed to the idea of "out and out" sex being the focus or central aspect of a couple's interactions.

Linda, 26, comments: "It bothers me that men want sex right from day one. It's not that I don't like sex, enjoy sex, want sex, but going to bed is not the first thing on my mind when I start dating someone."

For women in their twenties, an ideal man includes a lot more than sex. It is surprising that, despite all the freedom of expression and permissiveness of behavior tolerated in our society, women skirted the subject of sex when they thought of an ideal man. Not one woman in her twenties talked about an ideal man as someone who was a "great lay, terrific in bed." Nor did a single one make reference to the size or attractiveness of a man's genitals.

The women in our study also had great difficulty trying to imagine a nude image of their ideal man. We asked men and women to draw nude figures of their ideals. The directions were: "Please think of an ideal spouse. The quality of the drawing doesn't matter in the least. Draw a nude picture of this fantasy. Put in as many details as you can. Remember, we are *not* interested in how well you draw but in the realistic details."

(Before you read the results of this study, you might want to try the task yourself. You can then compare yourself to the participants in the study.)

Many men enthusiastically drew big breasts with clearly defined nipples, and some sketched in pubic hair. Some men who felt their drawings were weak put in labels and arrows in the direction of the genitalia. The women's faces were the least well-defined parts of the drawings. Hasty lines showed where nose, eyes, and ears belonged, although a remarkable number of men did put long hair on their ideals.

The difference between the men's and women's drawings was striking. Less than twenty percent of the women drew a penis with any clarity. Those who did make an attempt, roughly sketched in an elongated or round shape, which, allowing for lack of artistic talent, still bore little resemblance to an actual organ.

The vast majority of women were content with putting in tentative, scratchy lines in the crotch area. Although many women did put in lines indicating hair on a man's chest, relatively few drew any pubic hair. A notable exception was one young woman, a medical illustrator, who had no problems drawing a well-defined penis and testicles.

When we asked women about their hesitancy in drawing clearly identifiable male organs, some became embarrassed. Others told us they had no idea when they volunteered to be subjects they were going to participate in a pornographic study. A few accused us of an invasion of privacy because they had been asked to draw a nude male figure of their ideal.

Some women who felt uncomfortable with the instructions to draw a nude male insisted on putting bathing trunks or shorts on their ideal figures—anything to avoid confrontation with the male anatomy in such a public way.

Doreen, 23, explained her reluctance to draw a penis with any detail: "We're used to seeing naked women. Even women's magazines have photographs of nude women. But if I opened up my favorite magazine and found naked males all over the pages, I probably wouldn't continue to subscribe. I don't know why this is so. I guess conventions are hard to change."

Susan, 25, added: "I grew up with sisters. We had boy and girl dolls. They were identical except for the length of hair. The boy dolls didn't have a penis. I remember the first time I saw one. I baby-sat for a little boy and I was shocked. I must have been about 11. It occurred to me the other day that until I was 19 I had never seen an adult male naked. I had no real idea of what a man looked like in the nude. I bet there are a lot of women like myself, but they wouldn't dream of admitting their ignorance."

Men and women view their sex roles differently. As a result, problems between the sexes are bound to arise. Recognition of the difference in outlook between the sexes can be extremely important for young women in this age group who tend to be resentful and annoyed by young men's preoccupation with sex.

The ambivalence women may feel in discussing or identifying their ideals in sexual terms reflects, in part, the social values of our culture. Women, just as men, are faced with answering the question "Who Am I?" at different times in their lives. They manage beautifully with one exception—sex.

When it came to sex, a number of women admitted some confusion. Marilyn, 27, a computer analyst, said: "I still have doubts that I should be having sex before marriage. I come from a religious family. My mom always told me, 'Don't sleep with a man until you're married.' She was from the old school—virgin brides and all that.

"I can't count the number of times she warned me that men respected you for saying 'No.' I haven't the heart to tell her how old-fashioned she is. I would be sitting home if I made sure to always say 'no' with guys I dated seriously for a while."

Although Marilyn has sexual relations on occasion, there's still part of her that resists, part of her that questions whether she's doing the "right" thing: "My friends feel the same. It's really strange to me. I keep hearing and reading about all the women my age who haven't any hang-ups about having sex, sleeping with different guys, men they have no intentions of marrying, and yet, when I do it myself, I have these 'funny' feelings."

When it came to thinking about ideal men and sexual relations, today's women in this age group face far more of a dilemma than males. The simple explanation is that men haven't had to contend with radical changes in the codes for male sexual behavior. Male sexuality is pretty much the same today as it has been for centuries. There is no stigma attached to a man who has intercourse with a woman, or with many women, he would never dream of marrying.

This is definitely not the case for women. Many can't turn to their mothers for guidance. Nor do they have well-established ground rules to assist them in making decisions. In the past, the traditional female role vis-à-vis men was that women were supposed to be seductive and interesting, sexually arousing or provocative, as long as they didn't go "all the way."

Feminine identity was largely defined by sex appeal. For example, one only has to look at the popular movie queens of not so long ago. In movies women were not supposed to be thinking people. They were permitted a bit of cleverness or wittiness, but their main assets were full bosoms and rounded bottoms, which they capitalized on to catch a man. By and large, in the film story, the more overt their public sexy behavior, the more restrained they appeared in the bedroom prior to marriage. The heroines were typically bad girls outside and good girls inside.

Young women in the 1980s have reversed the traditional image. They are supposed to be unrestrained in the bedroom and yet their image to the world is one of a thinking, rational, professional person. These women don't want to be seen as objects of sex or passion. They want to relate to the men they meet as comrades and equal partners. And this wish runs counter to the ideal desires of young men who expect women to be eager and willing to enjoy the sexual freedoms acceptable in today's culture.

CHEMISTRY, NOT SEX

What women in their twenties see as ideal in a man as far as sex is concerned has a lot to do with good feelings and "chemistry." A majority of these women use words like "chemical reaction" to describe their ideal, whereas men spoke of ideals in terms of good old-fashioned sexual intercourse.

"What counts with me," said Anne, 24, "is the right chemistry. What I mean is magic, a feeling inside of me that this guy is right. I don't think about sex when I think about this feeling. I can have this 'chemistry' just holding hands or having a guy I like hold me in his arms. Sure there's sex, but chemistry has to be there. I think there's a difference. At least for me there is. The first time I had sex with a guy I liked, to be honest, it wasn't that much fun. I had more fun kissing him."

A number of women agreed with Anne. An ideal man wasn't just someone to have sex with. The sexual aspect grew out of a relationship. The relationship was based on love. Over and over, women in their twenties mentioned the importance of chemistry in their relations with an ideal man.

"Before I get into bed with someone," commented Roberta, 28, "there has to be something more than sex at stake. I remember the first time I had sex, I said to myself, 'What's the big deal?' I thought the experience would be some kind of mystical glow. I don't know what I really expected—perhaps bells to ring in my head. It wasn't like that at all. It wasn't even much fun—painful, in fact. I think it's different for men than for women. I think women need to practice learning how to have an orgasm. Men don't. I know the guy I had sex with the first time was having sex the first time himself. He was all exhausted and satisfied. I sure as hell wasn't.

"It got better with practice—the fun side. I went through a time when I thought it was going to be hopeless. I wasn't going to give up. Even now, if there isn't 'chemistry' nothing happens. And regardless of whether the guy really cares about me or not, sex *always* works for him. I have married friends who've told me they've never had an orgasm. They're still hoping. I think that's why when women describe an ideal man they don't think about sex. It just isn't that big a deal with a woman. We're physically different."

ROMANCE AND CANDLELIGHT

If women in their twenties don't stress the sex act, they definitely make a big point of the romantic part of a relationship. This means, in addition to the chemistry, having the right kind of setting and rarely does it mean a bedroom (as it does with men in this same age group). Women describe restaurants with candlelight, picnics in a park, twilight walks in woodsy settings. Many would agree with Elaine, 25, who said: "I picture myself sitting in a restaurant with candlelight. We're sort of both in shadows. We're holding hands. We touch. Maybe our legs touch. We're doing a lot of looking at each other. Looking is important. Looks can give you a delicious feeling, a real thrill, especially when you know you mean something to each other."

Romance fiction writers know full well that what counts with female readers are foreplay scenes: the chase, the looking, the furtive touching. Consummation of the sex act is not the titillating part. Men, on the other hand, enjoy scenes in films or books that include minute details of the act, down to the last bump, grind, grunt of orgasm, and ejaculation. Authors writing for men know better than to waste their readers' time on foreplay; they get right down to business with graphic sex scenes.

And so it's obvious that a wide chasm exists between the two sexes. An ideal woman for a man in his twenties is one who permits him to show his power and potency, and to prove his maleness without wasting time. Young women have a totally different view of what is ideal. Given the difference, it should come as no surprise that many young people in their twenties have problems trying to establish an intimate relationship. This is particularly true of modern young women who want to be valued for their brains and not for their breast size.

Certainly not all men are blatant about wanting to jump into bed for sex with women who arouse their lust. Many men learn to control their desires or, at best, learn discretion. They know how to engage in old-fashioned courtly hand-holding and long, lingering looks. However, others haven't learned diplomacy and come on much too strong too quickly. Such men often get rejected. Consciously or unconsciously, many women are turned off by a man who lacks sexual finesse and style even though he might otherwise fulfill their notion of an ideal mate. Both sexes have a better chance of success in a relationship once they agree on the ground rules about sexual activity. Through direct or indirect means both partners should get a clear idea of each others' attitudes, techniques, and desires.

Frances, 26, faced the problem of sexual incompatibility. For the past three years she's been living with Edward, 27. They met during college, dated sporadically, but didn't start a serious relationship until they became reacquainted a few years after graduation.

Their first dates were casual, warm, and pleasant—without sex. On the fourth date, after a summer afternoon's picnic, they wound up in Edward's apartment. One wonderful night together convinced them they should share living quarters.

Frances would like to get married. Edward isn't so convinced. According to him, Frances is a wonderful person. She has a great sense of humor and enjoys his jokes. They both like movies, junk food, and jogging, not necessarily in that order. Most importantly, Edward appreciates her good looks and terrific body. He recognized these "virtues" only after they started sleeping together regularly. Edward remembers his reaction to her in college: "When I first saw her all I saw was a bunch of clothes. She piled on all these sweaters. I was kind of surprised to discover what was underneath."

Edward admires Frances's personality, intellectual ability, and talents. Then why is he resisting marriage? "I don't think she's ever had a real orgasm. I think she's faked them. She goes through the motions. I know she likes me to touch her. I know she likes me to kiss her. But I've watched her and when it comes to going the whole way she doesn't show anything. I don't think she's had one. It cuts me up. I've had sex with a lot of women, a lot less attractive than Frances, a helluva lot less desirable, but they have something else, if you know what I mean. I satisfied them as much as they satisfied me.

"Before sex she'd be all fine. Then it's lost. She's not with it. I wouldn't ask her about it, though. I can't ask something like that. Besides, if I said anything, she'd probably tell me I'm crazy. She wouldn't admit the truth."

Edward's doubts are based on a number of cues. He mentions specifically the way Frances pops out of bed after sex and talks about some topic totally irrelevant to intercourse: "She'll ask me if I remembered to pick up my shirts from the laundry, or something like that."

Frances, on the other hand, said she enjoys sex to a degree: "I like to be held, to be kissed, touched." However, she admitted that when it came to the penis insertion she would freeze.

"I run scared. Even though I've taken precautions, I

worry. I keep thinking to myself, 'Is this the time I'll end up pregnant?' That's the last thing I want. It's different for a man. They don't have this worry. Nothing is a hundred percent sure. I won't take the pill. The side effects frighten me. Ed won't use a condom. I think that would help. I thought I'd try to talk to him about how I feel, but somehow all this reality takes the romance out of a relationship. It would make us feel like we're an old married couple having a down-to-earth discussion.

"It would be different, I know, if we married. Then if I became pregnant it wouldn't matter. I'm mixed up about it. It was a lot easier, believe me, for women in the past. They were supposed to be virgins until they married. They could keep guys dangling. And then they got married and pregnant. I don't want that either. I don't want kids now."

The potential threat of pregnancy appears to haunt many young women and to inject caution, concern, and sometimes even fear into their sex life. In some instances, it makes a difference in the kinds of pleasure they experience.

"I like sex," said Eileen, 24. "I think I'd like it a lot more—love it, even—if I wasn't frightened about pregnancy. No matter what anyone says, it has to be a lot different for a man and I think men *can* focus more on sex because they don't face this kind of worry. Nothing would be worse in my life than to face a problem I haven't bargained for—a pregnancy."

GETTING THE RIGHT MESSAGE ACROSS

Given the realities of a male's biology at this stage of development, it serves no purpose for young women in their twenties to be annoyed with the fact that males of this age seem to have sex on the brain. Sure, they may have other interests. They may enjoy concerts, theater, books, movies, bowling, and squash. But when it comes to women, the big sport is sex. A woman who captures the physical side of a man will have taken a giant step toward winning his love because she will have buttressed his new and somewhat shaky opinion of himself as a sexually potent male to the outside world, to himself, and, most importantly, to her.

In no way does this mean that a woman has to turn herself into a sex object or to give in to the sexual demands if she doesn't choose to. However, to ignore this fundamental aspect of males in their twenties is to play ostrich. Any hint or suggestion that a woman is not interested in the potency of the male she thinks she might like is going to spell doom to a relationship. Women need to have their egos flattered by being told they're desirable and attractive. Men need their egos bolstered by women's communicating the message that they're powerful and potent males. How a woman goes about getting this message across without jumping into bed at every free moment is obviously going to depend on her values, standards, and, above all, what she feels comfortable doing.

"GREEN EYES, BROAD SHOULDERS, BLONDE WAVY HAIR"

While it is true that some women may complain about the unfair sexual expectations of males in their twenties, in actuality women have much less of a problem trying to measure up to an ideal than do males. An astonishing number of women in this age group list specific traits of an ideal that rarely enter a male's thoughts.

Janice, 25, is an example: "Ever since I was a kid I had

Twenties / Establishing Identities

this idea in my mind that I would marry only a man who has curly brown hair and gray eyes." She realizes her image of an ideal may stem from a childhood storybook picture of a Prince Charming and admits to herself that she once rejected a date from a young man who had straight black hair and blue eyes.

Katie, 24, reports: "My ideal has green eyes, broad shoulders, blond wavy hair. He likes good food, dancing, and music. He wears chino pants, tweed jackets, and striped ties. If I ever run into him, I'll know right off who he is. I only hope he's smart enough to recognize that I'm the better half he's been waiting for."

One can well imagine Katie's reaction if an awkward young man wearing a suit with a white button-down shirt had the audacity to ask her out for an evening!

Karen, 26, is below average in height. With high heels on, she barely measures five feet. She insists she can relate only to six-footers. Her fantasy has gotten in the way of establishing relationships with men. On occasion when friends have introduced her to shorter men, she has reacted adversely, refusing to go out or at best accepting a date and behaving in a less-than-attractive manner.

The fantasies of these women are not shadowy phantom figures, but have definite shape and form. They come with specific traits: a certain color hair or eyes, for example (green eyes are often in demand). Bodies must be tall, slim, and muscular. As for facial features, women in their twenties are precise about these as well.

Some want their ideal to have long eyelashes. Others like the tilt in a man's nose. In fact, every single facial and bodily feature, with the glaring exception, of course, of sexual organs, is mentioned as part of the woman's ideal images.

On the other hand, rarely does the male in this age group come up with such clear-cut verbal descriptions. Kevin, 23, says: "Maybe an ideal should have long hair. I'm not really sure. Maybe short hair. I don't think hair matters all that much."

Peter, 26, thought he liked blondes, but then later he added, "I like girls with dark hair."

There was one notable exception to the vagueness of the men's descriptions, and that was body weight. John, 25, gave a typical response when he said, "My ideal has to be slim. She's got to have a terrific figure."

The vast majority of males in their twenties agree on slimness, great bodies, and pleasing or attractive figures. Not one man carried on about the length of a woman's eyelashes or whether she had curls in her hair or her hair was straight. All these fine details were virtually ignored. In fact, if one just listened to the descriptions of a male's ideal woman, one would have trouble identifying that woman in a crowd.

Women may complain about males in this age group emphasizing sexual traits; however, the men have an equal right to gripe. Not every man is handsome; not every man has long eye lashes or aquamarine-colored eyes; not every man has broad shoulders setting off a six-foot-plus frame. Many men in their twenties are nice-looking guys but don't, as they will readily admit themselves, necessarily resemble a handsome prince in a fairy tale picturebook.

The reason women are careful to list specific features in an ideal mate is that they are much more interpersonally oriented. Their concern is with social interactions and the evaluations of others. Women in their twenties are extremely conscious of peer reactions.

Caroline, 24, noted: "It's no different now from the time

I was in high school. I know I'm judged by my friends. That's how I judge other people. I remember the gossip when someone went out with a homely guy. Homely girls wouldn't date homely guys, at least if they thought others at school would see them. Even if the boy was the nicest kid in the world, he had trouble getting a date. I had a friend who, rather than go to the prom with this freaky-looking guy in our class, stayed home. I thought at the time she was crazy. But nothing has changed! When I try to fix up friends of mine with guys I know, the first question they ask is, 'Is he good-looking?' I've never had anyone ask me about personality first or if the guy is nice."

Dee, 28, would love to get married. If one listened to her during the interview, one might conclude that no single men exist in her age bracket. This is far from the case, of course. It is true, however, there are not hordes of men over six feet tall who shave twice a day because she can't stand scratchy cheeks, who have social graces that are right for every occasion and flashing blue eyes.

Melissa commented that she feels badly about her brother David, who is 29 and has an M.B.A. and a well-paid job. "He spends Saturday nights listening to tapes by himself. He dresses well and he's got a nice personality when he feels relaxed. He's shy. But that's not what turns girls off. I know they think he's homely. He's not gorgeous. I know that. But right now he feels so vulnerable. He's scared about calling someone up for a date and doesn't want me to fix him up."

Melissa, a wise woman in her mid-thirties, told her brother, "Just wait a couple of years. You'll be a partner in the firm. The same girls who wouldn't look at you twice will be older, and they'll be crawling all over themselves to get your attention."

Just as women are conscious that males in their twenties are interested in sex, men, too, are aware that women in the same age group prize handsomeness. In meeting women's high standards, men face problems women simply don't encounter. Women can buy sexy clothing, and wear makeup to enhance their sex appeal.

However, for cultural reasons, men can't do much about radically altering their appearance. By and large it isn't acceptable for men to wear makeup to enhance features or minimize others; they can't, or don't, put on eyelashes simply because they know women like long-lashed men; they don't change the color of their hair readily. Nor can they alter their height significantly simply by putting on another pair of shoes. Given the restraints of our society, many men in their twenties do fall far short of women's ideals. But, in the face of their disappointments, they would do well to keep in mind Melissa's remarks to her brother: A few more years and they can be round, short, balding, and blue, green, or brown-eyed, and they'll still have quite a field of women to choose from as women's concepts of an ideal gradually change.

A GOOD LISTENER WITH A BEAUTIFUL FACE

It would be quite a misconception to assume that all males in their twenties have only sex on their minds. They have many other concerns as well—such as careers, and worries about the directions their lives will take. They have a growing awareness that they are no longer free-wheeling adolescents and must take a position in the adult world. Many aren't sure how to go about this. They feel on shaky ground insofar as their careers are concerned. They need and want assurance from the outside world about their potential and abilities. A few short years before, parents served this role. However, now the male wants those pats on the back and the unquestioning faith in his future to come from a caring, understanding, thoughtful, sincere, super-interested female who, in addition to being a terrific listener, is endowed with all the sexual qualities any man could possibly desire. To sum it up, an ideal woman for a man in his twenties is someone who has an inexhaustible ability to listen, a beautiful head and sexy body.

After sex, the top traits for a male in his twenties had to do with **LISTENING SKILLS**. This doesn't mean two-way communication. These men want listeners, *not* talkers. She must listen to his confusions, his doubts. She must listen to him talk about sports, his car if he owns one, and problems with his family. The role of the woman in her twenties is to sit there wide-eyed and to say "uhuhuh" at appropriate times, mostly to indicate that she hasn't fallen asleep.

Occasionally, the wise woman will ask a question more as a device to keep the conversation moving forward than to add to her store of information.

Sharon, 25, described what it is like to be on a date with a man in her age bracket: "He'll begin with a quick question about me, like is my job fun or something ridiculous like that. And then we move on to him. To his problems, his concerns. Once in a while I'll say something like, 'Gee that sounds awful,' or 'I really can't imagine someone doing that. Is that really what happened?' I have a whole bunch of stock phrases. What I say isn't all that important but *how* I say it is. If we're having dinner together, I'll lean over and shake my head or something like that, make a little sound with my lips. I think if just once I met someone who sat back and asked me what I did and wanted to hear more, I'd fall over in a dead faint."

It's a burden for young women in their twenties to play

this all-understanding, listening role. They, too, want to have someone listen to them. The fact is, they're going to have to wait a few years for the men in their own age bracket to grow into this kind of role. Either that, or they're going to have to settle for dating and marrying much older men who, as we'll see, realize that listening and being listened to are important for a relationship.

It may be helpful for women to remember that, while men in their twenties are egocentric, they are not selfish or mean. Their egocentrism has a totally different basis. It stems from an honest worry and concern about their future.

Victor, 25, described his feelings: "I think of where I'm going to be ten years from now. I get bothered. Then I say, 'What the hell.' I can't get that psyched up about the future when I'm not sure what I'll be doing a month from now.

"Some days I think maybe I'll stay in sales. I think I might make it. I get along. Then other days I ask myself why don't I walk out and do what I really want to do—stock car racing. I think a lot about that. I like working around cars."

Victor's notions of spending his life around stock cars makes his girl friend bristle with anger: "He likes to play. If he did that seriously that would be fine. But he's not serious. One day it's stock car racing, and the next day it'll be surfing. He just doesn't want to grow up. He's like he was in high school. He has such super talents, but sometimes, when he thinks about what he's going to do with his life, he's worse than a kid."

Victor's indecision is upsetting to a mature woman of 25 who knows where she's going and what she wants from life. And that's very much true of women in this age group

Twenties / Establishing Identities

today. This generation of women are often years beyond their male counterparts both socially and developmentally. The women's movement has made a tremendous impact on women's lives in more ways than just opening doors to careers and educational opportunities. By changing developmental patterns, it has also thrown women totally out of sync with men of the same age.

Today there is a far greater proportion of young women in their twenties who aren't married, who are finding it difficult to meet young men, who gravitate to older men, who find that men their own age are hard to meet and hard to establish relationships with on a steady basis. To put it somewhat differently, what this means is that many young women today are organized, purposeful, directed, motivated, educated, and feel, many times, at a loss with males in their twenties who are still floundering or indecisive and thinking about their career directions.

Modern young women have thrown over traces of the past and are settling into lives unheard of for women a generation ago. To cite one example, we might consider young women on their way to colleges or universities today. It often comes as a shock to them when they hear that colleges were not always viewed as places where young women could be trained or educated for productive positions in society. The purpose of college for many women of a generation or so ago was to serve as a mating ground— to bring them to a place where they could easily meet young men who might be suitable husbands.

We remember teaching at a large midwestern university in the years prior to the women's movement, and foolishly giving out assignments during winter carnival week. The men didn't object to the assignments. However, the women in the class marched up to us and told us that we had erred and no way were they going to do the work when they had more important things to do in preparation for the big festivities. One young woman, head of the delegation, asked if we understood why she was in college. "To meet a husband" was her reply to her own question.

The dialogue seems absurd today. We assure you it was very real at the time and our bet is that the daughters of these same women are now in school for very different reasons.

Young women in the past may have pursued some academic interests, but they also chased boys to insure that by the time they graduated they had met a suitable spouse. There was no problem being in sync. Today, the situation is totally different. Women in their twenties are generally more mature than males in the same age group and when you add to this direction and a goal, the gap between young men and women inevitably has to grow bigger in terms of social development.

And so it is that women today portray ideal men in much the same way that they envision themselves. They admire career or goal-oriented young men. They value sensitive, interesting, patient souls who will be good providers someday for the families these young women see as part of their destiny. Furthermore, women in their twenties want attention. In fact, there is an interesting dichotomy here in the wishes of these women. On the one hand, we have determined that the successful, talented, reality-oriented woman in this age group wants a career, not just a job. On the other hand, she still has a strong romantic side. She is still the same woman who feels as Jeanie does: "I want a husband who sees me as number one all the way. No ifs, no buts, no maybes. I'm number one in his eyes. This means valentines on Valentine's Day and flowers on

Twenties / Establishing Identities 51

my birthday. I want someone who will be crazy about me. That's my ideal."

The romantic man for this woman isn't someone who just whispers passionate words in candlelight settings. Romantic feelings include more than passion and this "more" is a respect and appreciation for the young woman's talents and interests.

The need for attention creates a real problem for the twenties. Both sexes demand it. Both want to be number one! It is clearly a "me" decade. If women in the past thought about catering to men, women today think of catering to themselves. Not once did any young woman in her twenties say anything remotely like, "My ideal man is someone I will be crazy about. My ideal is someone I love." The phrasing was, always "someone who cares about me."

This attitude reflects the fundamental change that has taken place for women today: the orientation to serve others has been replaced by the recognition that women are individuals in their own right. And it is this shift that causes problems between the sexes; men in their twenties don't see the world in the same way. Their lives haven't been turned around in the way that women's lives have. They continue to live socially and developmentally much as their fathers and their grandfathers before them did.

Although men and women have different developmental needs in their twenties and thus fantasize vastly dissimilar ideals, all is not lost for the decade. There are plenty of times when the male tires of self-indulgent monologues and is willing to shift roles for a bit. He enjoys joking around and having fun. "A sense of humor," "fun to be with," and "laughs a lot" were all traits highly valued by both men and women. Fantasy people had wreaths of smiles on their faces, knew a good joke, and wanted to entertain and be entertained—in short, fun images are crucial.

"IT'S KNOWING THAT YOU BELONG TOGETHER"

The final—but not least—trait valued by young women is intimacy, a word that simply never cropped up in discussions with men in their twenties. Intimacy, as we shall see, is desired by women of all ages and has different meanings at different stages. For a woman in her twenties, however, the term has a special connotation. Intimacy means a closeness, the kind of understanding that comes with just perhaps a look, a touch of the hand, the invisible bond between two people that is, in part, physical as well as psychological.

Young women define the term as a special sense of belonging. Larissa, 27, says that "It's knowing that you belong to each other even when you're not together."

For young women, then, intimacy is an extremely important feeling, and their interpretation of the word is vastly different from men of the same age. Intimacy for males has pretty much one meaning—sex. However, in general, they don't even use the word—it isn't part of their working vocabulary. When pressed for a definition of intimacy, the typical answer is like Rob's, 27, who said: "I think it means for me who I'm sleeping with on a regular basis." This comment was a straightforward, simple definition of a term that for women communicated complex and significant emotional feelings.

Women in their twenties look at intimacy in a starry-eyed fashion. Their voices even take on a softer timbre. For women, intimacy—more than sex, more than hugs in bed, more than even that candlelight dinner at a favorite restaurant—brings a rosy glow to their cheeks and a glint to their eyes. Being intimate with a man makes sense out of the bonding that comes with a marriage or a relationship. Intimacy makes sense of life, gives it a form and a purpose. Later, perhaps, the intimacy will be extended to a child, but in the childless stage women turn to their mates.

"I know intimacy for me," said Adrienne, 27, "means that I am never lonely. I can be alone. That's different. But it means that, even when I'm physically alone, if I have an intimate relationship with a man, I carry that feeling inside of me and it affects whatever I'm doing. It just makes me feel warm and secure. I am never, never lonely. I never, never have that cold feeling inside that can be so awful—so very depressing. And maybe a little frightening, too."

We've noted a number of gaps between the way women and men perceive ideal mates, and it is manifestly clear that the need for intimacy, as well as the significance intimacy has in a relationship and in life, is vastly different for the two sexes. Men simply don't crave this kind of intimacy with a woman. This doesn't mean that the man in his twenties rejects closeness. But on no occasion did any man mention that warm glow, that feeling of intensity that stayed with him regardless of whether or not he was with the person who meant a lot to him. Leonard, 27, is an example: "My girlfriend means a lot to me. Do I think about her when I'm not with her? Sure—some. I mean, she crosses my mind when I'm at work. But if I'm really involved in a job I'm doing, then I can't say I do think about her. I'm not distracted that way. I think I have pretty good powers of concentration."

Women, on the other hand, often confess to thinking

a great deal about a fiancé, a husband, or someone with whom they are having a relationship: "Joe is on my mind constantly," said Francine, 24, who recently became engaged. "I'll be doing my job and really think I'm interested in it and then it hits me that I'm going with Joe and we're going to be married. I sometimes wonder what other people would say if they knew that when I'm talking to them about their mortgages I'm really thinking about him. I think women go through this phase—that is, thinking about guys all the time—until they settle down and get used to the idea they're married."

When it comes to an intimate relationship, women in their twenties have to be patient just as men in this age group have to be tolerant. It's not a question of despair. It's a question of time. Men in their twenties are becoming their own persons; they are discovering who they are and within a short time they'll be ready for some of the giving qualities women desire. On the other hand, perhaps women this age might sit back and take stock of their needs and desires. Some had best stay on hold for a while. Patience might be the name of the meeting game.

LIVING IN SYNC

The key to living in sync is the mutual awareness and satisfaction of each other's needs. As we have seen, men and women in their twenties are primarily concerned with establishing their identities in the adult world. But the typical pattern of needs for men and women is likely to be somewhat different. He, for example, may need to be assured that he's a powerfully potent male, both in terms of his sexuality as well as his capacity to succeed in the world of work. She, on the other hand, may need to be assured that she is a valued, intensely desired person, not only because of her physical attractiveness, but also because of her intelligence, her personality, talents, and abilities. When husband and wife are aware of each other's needs, they can foster and reinforce each other's psychological development, and as a result, grow together in sync.

THE PRINCIPLE OF RECIPROCAL REACTION

Understanding, of course, is not enough. To live in sync, this understanding must be reflected in the ways that a couple interacts with each other. It's not only the behavior of the husband or of the wife that makes a difference; it's their *interaction* that is important.

It is abundantly clear from our study that a husband and wife at any given age probably have somewhat different psychological needs. A couple living in sync recognizes and appreciates these differences and, in the light of them, interacts in ways that complement each other. This means that husband and wife don't necessarily behave in exactly the same way to each other, because each of them needs something different from the other person. Husband and wife behave differently, but *reciprocally,* in satisfying each other's needs.

Reciprocal reaction is the core of happy and enduring marriages. Satisfying your spouse's needs increases the probability that your spouse will satisfy your needs. Thus, the man in his twenties who clearly conveys to his wife that he values, cherishes, and respects her, not only because of her physical attributes but also because of her other qualities, will in turn be most likely to elicit from his wife the assurance that he is a powerfully potent male. As a consequence of this reciprocal reaction, each person becomes a primary source of strength and security for the other, supporting and promoting each other's development as individuals, and at the same time, strengthening the psychological bonds of their marriage.

THE THIRTIES

The Status Decade

Only one day separates a 29-year old from the thirties decade, but, in terms of feelings, the twenty-four hours symbolize an awesome shift in attitudes and values. For both men and women, the 30th birthday is a giant step into the mature world. Adolescence and the twenties were also steps along the way to adulthood. However, as Ted, 31, said, "Somehow when I turned 20 after 19, it didn't seem to matter all that much. With 30 I felt different. I felt like I was moving toward middle-age. I'm no longer a kid in my eyes or in the eyes of other." For a fair number of men and women, the carefree spirit of the twenties suddenly is overshadowed by mature feelings, worries, and concerns. In terms of an average lifespan, 30 years old is just below the halfway mark. Perhaps this recognition creates a sudden awareness of destiny, a realization that one is moving along in the aging process.

A GOOD-PAYING JOB

How much do people in their thirties change in terms of their ideal spouses? In one word, the answer is dramatically! In some respects the descriptions of men and women in their twenties have very little relationship to those of the thirties. The comments of Brian, 34, are shared by an overwhelming majority of men in this age bracket. When asked what was the number one trait he wanted to see in an ideal spouse, his immediate answer was, "a good-paying job."

His wife's paycheck is something Brian treasures and respects. Brian was not being completely facetious in his response. He explained: "I love my wife. We were married when we were both 23. I've never regretted my decision, and I don't think she has either."

They laughed their way through the experience of living in a miserable one-room walk-up apartment. When they were 27, they bought their first new furniture and were afraid to sit on the couch because they thought it might wear out before they could add other pieces. At the end of seven years, they had two children, a few more pieces of furniture, and a lot of bills to pay.

"Suddenly we felt like Noah's ark. We had two kids, two budgies, two cars. I remember my 30th birthday. Some buddies of mine asked me to play ball that morning. I thought about going. I knew Ginny was planning something for me. Billy was driving her crazy. He was 2. She was pregnant and tired. I felt like I was being pulled down in quicksand. For a moment there I wanted out. I think Ginny felt the same way. Then the baby was born. Ginny's mother moved near us to take care of the kids and Ginny went back to work. She's a nurse and could arrange her hours. I tell you, a load was lifted from my back. It used to be hell the first of the month. No way did I see how we were going to make it. That's all changed with Ginny working. I'm not kidding when I say an ideal wife at my age is one with a good-paying job."

Men in their twenties can afford to ignore or be cavalier about an ideal spouse's earning ability. The realities of mortgages, kids' shoes, baby-sitters, lawn mowers, and all the other paraphernalia that goes with the thirties nesting stage of life seem far-removed. They can dream about breasts and bed play and not worry about overdrawn bank accounts and grass seed. Men in their twenties, even those who marry in the decade, enjoy the luxury of focusing on fun and games.

Does this mean that owning a Gold credit card is one way to the heart of a man in his thirties? It certainly may not be the only way, but one can't minimize the importance of a woman's income when ==over seventy-five percent of the men in this age group== ranked earning capabilities somewhere in the top five desired traits of their ideal wife.

Roger, 32, is not married. He has a new girl friend he thinks he might get serious about. "We've been seeing each other for about six months. The problem is I'm not so sure we'd be right for each other in the long haul."

According to Roger, Martha is fun, sexy, intelligent, and shares many of his interests. Why, then, the reservations or doubts about marriage? The truth is that Roger is disturbed because Martha doesn't have any career goals: "She has a dead-end job and is not at all dissatisfied. Her raises are regular. She gets a Christmas bonus, which is all fine and good, but the job doesn't lead anywhere. Ten years from now on she could be doing the same thing and making just about the same amount of money."

However, worse than the job's not having a future is Martha's total indifference to a career. Her plan, which she has not hidden from Roger, is to work for a few years after they are married, save enough money for a downpayment on a house, get pregnant, and quit her job. She doesn't believe in working when children are small. This would mean, since they plan to have several children, Roger would have to earn enough to support them all for at least ten years.

He worries about assuming this kind of major responsibility. "Maybe it was OK years ago. It's different now. It costs a fortune to have kids." He has noted the awesome amounts quoted in magazines as being necessary to support a child from birth through college. "I've looked at advertisements for apartments and houses. On my salary I think Martha is in fantasy land to think we could afford to have her not work. If she had a job, there wouldn't be any problem. Maybe she could cut back once we had kids, but another income would still be necessary. I see her point about not working full-time when kids are small. But I can't see her staying home full-time as a way of life."

Roger brought up the subject of women's liberation: "Where has it led to? I mean, sometimes I get these lectures from Martha how she expects a guy to pitch in fifty-fifty with housework and kids. In the next breath, she tells me she has no intentions of having kids just to ship them off to day-care centers or hiring someone to take care of them. There's no reason why she shouldn't have a job—some kind of career. I don't know if I can ever earn that kind of money to support all she wants."

Thirties / The Status Decade

Many men in their thirties are married or planning marriage. Those who married in their twenties and whose wives delayed having children suddenly find themselves interested in starting families. The carefree couple's life is suddenly coming to an end. Those with young children face increased costs of clothing and feeding: "When a 2-year-old's sneakers cost almost as much as mine, you better believe it when I say a number one virtue in an ideal wife is a paycheck," Mike, 33, commented.

In a study we completed several years ago about mother-infant relationships, it was interesting to note that some fifty percent of the women interviewed worked either part- or full-time. And of that number about half worked at the insistence of their husbands. Melanie, 34, told us: "I was happy to stay home. I loved my career. I liked the money but I thought it better for the baby if I was there all the time. It was my husband who pushed me back into a job."

In terms of women's working, the women's movement has come full circle. Perhaps at the outset there was resistance on the part of men, but this is definitely not the case today. One man we spoke to commented that once men caught on to the advantages of women's having jobs they would be all for women working. "That is as long as they also take care of the house and the kids and the pets," added another. In another instance, one of the men remembered that when his mother wanted to work outside the house his father was devastated: "He was embarrassed that his wife worked and thought maybe relatives would say he couldn't support the family. That isn't the case now. The truth is, I can't support kids, cars, a mortgage, and my wife's clothing on my salary."

BUT NOT TOO MUCH MONEY

Although men are supportive of women's working, when it comes to the salaries or the amounts women are to contribute toward family expenses, the men hold divided opinions. More than half the men feel that an ideal wife is one who has a well-paying job but that her salary should be lower than a man's, even when the nature of the work is the same.

Andrew, 35, is proud of his wife's computer skills: "She's a great programmer. Twice in a couple of years she's been promoted. She's in a training program now on the managerial level." His enthusiasm for her career recently has been tempered by the worry that his wife's paycheck is edging perilously close to his own.

"I don't like it," he admitted. Although a vast majority of men in their thirties liked the idea of working wives, when a woman's earning power and status matched or exceeded the male's, discomfort and resentment tempered the pleasure.

The major exceptions to this belief are men who enjoy exceptional status or who are acknowledged as successes even though their earning power doesn't equal their wives'. Chris, 36, works as a researcher in a biology laboratory. His work has been recognized by people in the field, and he is author of a number of professional articles. He is currently working on a book that will, as he noted, sell a few hundred copies to a specialized audience. His 34-year-old wife is in public relations. Her salary is twice as much as Chris's and eventually will be even higher. Chris isn't concerned, but he feels his situation is special because his work has more status than his wife's does. "I'm not sure how I would feel if this weren't the case," he admitted. "Her earning more money and having more prestige."

"DO I GIVE UP MY JOB TO FIND A HUSBAND?"

Ideal men for women in their thirties also have to have good jobs, and potential or present status. This is particularly true for women who are professional or who are on specific career tracks, as opposed to women who have ordinary jobs.

For a number of women in their thirties, finding an ideal spouse who measures up to them in career goals poses one of the major problems of the 1980s. Sandra, 32, is a prime example of this particular group. She's a vice president of a major corporation and commands a handsome salary. In the mornings, a company limo picks her up at her apartment house and returns her to the door at the end of the day.

"Where do I find a guy?" is her present lament. "The men I meet who are my age don't have high salaries or equivalent status. Companies are out luring women, and promoting them faster than they do men. Sure, there is the occasional bright-eyed wonder, but for the most part, young men in their thirties aren't vice presidents. Guys I meet run scared. Do I give up my job to find a husband? Definitely not. Do I hide the amount of my paycheck and lie about what I do?"

Several men who were potentially interesting became defensive when they found out where Sandra worked and the nature of her position. One, in particular, a teacher in a secondary school, was frank with Sandra. He said it would bother him as a male to have a wife who earned more and held a more important position. Sandra has finally decided she won't let men know what she does until some kind of relationship is established between them: "I'm not going to lie, but I've got to do more on Saturday nights than sit in front of a VCR."

MONEY AND STATUS

Although many women disclaim primary interest in a man's current salary, they are interested in his potential earning power. Judy noted: "I know that I want a family, a house. I can't see myself marrying a man who wouldn't eventually be able to provide for a family. If I have kids, I might want to stop working while they were young. I wouldn't be able to do this if my husband didn't have a good job or make enough money to support a house and family."

Women in their thirties don't ignore status. Men can earn less money than they do. That is fine with the woman. Eighty percent of them, however, want the man's job or profession to be equal in status to theirs and the vast majority have no objection if the man's work has greater status in the eyes of society. In fact, many prefer this.

Pauline, 31, commented: "When I married Tom I had a much higher paying job and more status than he did. But we both knew that this uneven balance was temporary. Eventually his job matched mine, and I don't doubt he will go a lot further because I'll probably take a break when we have kids. Frankly it would bother me if Tom had a lower status job and salary permanently. I think it's part of the culture. It's OK if a woman's job is less valuable, but in a marriage, there's trouble when the tables are reversed. I've seen it happen time and time again. I have a friend whose husband is an artist. He doesn't sell much. He may never make much money. She's a manager in a corporation and gets a huge salary. They've never had any problems because everyone respects her husband as an artist. But let me tell you, if he were just an ordinary kind of guy, drifting around in jobs, that marriage wouldn't last a day."

FIFTY-FIFTY ON THE HOME FRONT

Although women may accept a man as having more job status and a greater salary, almost without exception, women in their thirties insist on equality in every other aspect of the relationship. An ideal man is someone who respects a woman, sees her as equal in every way, and shares all the responsibilities in the relationship, including domestic chores, and caring for the children.

Women in their twenties rarely mention equality as a virtue of an ideal in contrast to their counterparts in their thirties, who consistently include it among their top priorities. The phrases used over and over again were "respect for my work," "understands I have a career," "sees women as equal." The key word is respect. The women are on guard against any behavior on the part of males that smacks of chauvinism.

It is interesting to note that the definition of equality differs according to a woman's marital status. Single women, like Elissa, say an ideal man must see her job as being just as important as his. Married women, on the other hand, even if they are working and have careers, define equality in terms of domestic responsibilities.

Lisa, 34, has been married for five years. Childless, she said an important trait in an ideal man is his willingness to pitch in and do his share around the house: "We both have jobs. Our marriage would never work if I had to do everything. We had a problem about this and almost split. I never thought a marriage could end because two people fought over who was going to take out the garbage on Monday nights. But the issue was a matter of principle. We were ending up in traditional roles, and I simply wasn't going to take it. We each had to carry our fair share. Maybe it will change when we have kids. I don't think it should. Frankly this one point worries me. I've worked too hard and too long for my career to throw it all over. I think if it happened, that I was put into the role of domestic slave, I would rebel. I'd walk out."

Not all women spoke as forcefully, but the message remains the same. Women in their thirties, regardless of status—single, married, childless, or with children—had a lot to say about equality on the domestic level.

THE AWESOME IDEAL WOMEN

Men in their thirties, almost without exception, never mention any form of equality among the desired traits in an ideal spouse. What these men do prize is a woman who is energetic, intelligent, hard-working, sensitive, trusting, a good mother, a good housekeeper. She doesn't have to be beautiful, and she doesn't have to be the gorgeous sex symbol of all times. Presentable, yes, but one had the feeling in talking with the men that if she had a super paycheck, ran the house beautifully, managed the kids, and had a hot dinner on the table, certain things, like how she looked in a bikini, could be overlooked.

In many ways the list of traits expected of an ideal woman for a man in his thirties is awesome. Domestic abilities, career potential, conversational skills are only part of the picture. Men in this age group add the adjectives fun-loving and adventuresome to round out their portrait of the super-woman. More than at any other age, the expectancies of these males match the super-woman syndrome, a popular female image in today's media.

Barry, 35, was asked how he could possibly expect a woman to be on time for a meeting at her job, get the laundry and shopping done, breast-feed the baby, entertain business associates of his while also managing to paint the kitchen and perhaps help repair the computer he just bought? For Barry all these skills were part of the role he *assumed* modern young women desired. For him, the ability to do all these things mean a woman is liberated!

In many ways a male in his thirties is a demanding person when it comes to his ideal woman. Is he being selfish? Is he being narrow-minded? Is he taking women's liberation to the extreme? The answer to all these questions is, no! Why, then, the desire for such a remarkable person as a spouse?

AN AGE OF BECOMING

In order to understand the portrait of the ideal woman for a man in his thirties, we must consider what is going on in the man's life at this age. By and large these men are describing a broad spectrum of virtues and traits they see as necessary to complement their own lives. They are beginning a course of settling in and settling down. It is also a time which Erik Erikson, a renowned psychologist, identified as "generativity." The man is busy generating a career, generating a family, living out the self-promises and goals he began to define for himself in his twenties. Males in their thirties are "becoming": fulfilling an identity, carving a niche, a career, a place for themselves in society. A male in this age group is a very busy person. The qualities he demands in an ideal wife parallel his own energies and interests. The interpretation that he is a demanding, egocentric, chavinistic male is far from the truth.

Men in their thirties describe an ideal wife as one who manages a house and children, with ease and graciousness. Ideal wives can entertain business associates, clip a bush in the yard, and repaint the kitchen if necessary and also make sure the kids get to their dentist appointments on time. All these activities go on while at the same time the ideal wife has a responsible, well-paying job. Super-mom and super-wife emerge from the portraits these men describe in an ideal.

STRAINS ON EQUALITY

Keith, 36, defended his emphasis on the wide-ranging talents he would like to see in an ideal wife: "I believe in equality. My wife knows that. I'd like to help around the house more. My hours are a killer. I simply can't get away as much as I would like to. When I get my business established, I'm hoping things will ease off. My wife knew this. She was the one who encouraged me to go out on my own. When I worked for someone else, it wasn't the same. At the end of the workday I was more or less finished. Sure there were times I had to take work home. Now that I work for myself it's everynight at my desk. I can't close the door at the end of the day. The door to the office is never closed in my mind."

His wife, however, is irritated: "Keith isn't helping. He forgets I have a full-time job and the house and the kids. He thinks he's the only one who's overworked." Jan feels that Keith could help her out more. An ideal man in her mind is one who charges along in his own career, somehow manages to find the same energy for domestic affairs that women are automatically assumed to possess. Many women share Jan's reaction and, with the women in their thirties terms like "respect," "appreciation of a woman's job," and "sharing of responsibilities" appear more and more often among the top choices of qualities.

LIFE IN THE THIRTIES IS A SERIOUS BUSINESS

In contrast to the fun and games mood of the twenties, a serious tone enters the descriptions of an ideal man for women in their thirties. They are aware of things to be done and responsibilities. A prime example of this seriousness is the mention of ideal traits that have to do with parenting. This is the case whether or not the woman is single, married, has children, or is childless.

Christine, 33, is single. At the moment, she doesn't have any serious interest in a man, but indicated that her ideal would have to love children, dogs, a home, be a generous, sensitive, understanding parent. He would also have to have a sense of responsibility and be a hard worker.

If one considers the qualities Christine describes as ideal, it's evident that they all add up to being a good father—a family man. This is exactly what Christine noted in her own self-appraisal. She said that dating in her thirties is quite different from when she was in her twenties. Then, a good-looking, sociable man satisfied her concept of an ideal man. Now, however, she finds that the question "Will he make a good father?" often crosses her mind when she enters a new relationship: "In my twenties, I never thought about having kids. I never particularly saw myself settling down. Women who did that belonged to my mother's generation. For me it was important to be out, getting my advanced degrees, having the fancy job."

Suddenly, without awareness, Christine became consumed by what we have termed "baby hunger," the longing for a baby. In fact one of the major reasons that women's descriptions of ideal men shift dramatically in the thirties has to do with this biological urge to have a child.

Why the thirties? There is no mystery why baby hunger, which can, of course, occur at any age, suddenly takes on a special urgency at that age. Women realize that their time for having children doesn't stretch on endlessly. They are quickly approaching the critical cut-off point of the forties. For someone like Christine who isn't married and is 33 years old, this means that she has to meet someone soon, get to know him, get married, and become pregnant all in the space of a few years. She's justifiably concerned about what she has to accomplish in a relatively short span of time.

Baby hunger is a very real phenomenon, an inescapable longing, a physical as well as an emotional desire that in many instances causes women in their thirties to describe ideal spouses not as potential husbands, but as potential fathers. For example, Madeline, 36, said: "I never dreamt I would consider what a man earned as an important ideal trait. But I want a baby, and I don't want to work. Money is important. I chose a man who could support me. It was definitely a factor in my decision. Of course, I loved him. Would I have loved him the same if he was flat broke and didn't have a job and I couldn't become pregnant because there wasn't any money to support a family? In all honesty, I don't think I would have."

In contrast, far fewer men list being a good mother as an important criteria of an ideal wife. Some sixty percent of the men, however, do cite such terms as good homemaker and good cook as important. Although men want families and want to become parents, the inner compelling force that hits women in this decade simply does not generally occur in men. They may want children, but do not experience anything remotely like baby hunger. A man doesn't consider a woman an ideal simply because he thinks she'll be a good mother to his children.

THE WAY SHE PUTS HERSELF TOGETHER

Men in their twenties stress a perfect body, full bosom, curvacious hips, lovely face. In contrast, men in their thirties are much less demanding in terms of physical beauty.

Walter, 33, is quite typical of many men his age in his definition of what he means by good-looking: "There's the type of women in magazines, all doctored up for presentation. Great to look at them. They're not the real world. My wife is beautiful for me. She might not be for another guy. She's very nice-looking. She takes care of herself. Keeps herself in shape. She's not a movie star. She'd be the first to admit that. But I'm not God's gift to women, either. My wife looks good to me. I look good to her. That's what counts."

Like many men, Walter values and admires the way a woman puts herself together, more than he insists upon intrinsic physical perfection. This changing of demands as far as physical beauty is concerned has tremendous importance to women. Elizabeth, 33, said: "It hit me the other day that I didn't start a real social life until after 30. I wondered why. I used to think it was me, what I said, what I did. Then one day it hit me. Guys don't expect the same thing they expect in their twenties."

MORE THAN JUST PERFORMANCE IN BED

Men in their twenties are impatient. They don't want to waste time before getting into bed with their ideals.

However, the maturity of thirties males is evident in their ability to wait for gratification. One of the signs of maturity is being able to handle delayed gratification. A child needs that lollipop immediately as a reward for good behavior. He can't wait. The male in his twenties also isn't very good at waiting, particularly when it comes to sexual gratification.

But by his thirties, the male is more poised, more assured, more in control of himself, and he can wait. He doesn't need to go to bed on a first date. He may not even need this kind of reward on a second or a third date. He has learned to be patient.

This ability to hold off sex can be a welcome relief for some women in their thirties. Maureen, 33, recalls how men in their twenties would come up to her apartment and immediately look for the bed. "I knew what was on their minds. Men in their thirties can sit down like adults and talk."

It's not that males in their thirties don't enjoy sex, want sex, and view sexual pleasure an important part of life. It's just that they realize that sex is not always the center of everything. There are other aspects to a male-female relationship which are worthy of cultivating.

This recognition that women are more than sexual playmates has a lot to do with the developmental stage of the thirties. Men in their twenties are egocentric. The world revolves around them and their concerns. However, by the time a man is 30, he is more put together. He probably knows what career he will have. He is thus more confident in himself as a person and has less need for constant reassurance about his image as a sexually potent male. Given his personal self-confidence, he can afford the time and energy to turn outwards, to think about another person's needs.

Thirties / The Status Decade

For the first time, perhaps since kindergarten, men in their thirties realize that females are more than just bodies. Thus they don't always have to measure the size of a woman's breasts to determine whether she's going to make a fun companion for an evening or for life.

They also want to be able to talk to a woman. Sharing is a major concern. A man in his thirties wants and needs to share thoughts, interests, feelings. Thus, when lovemaking comes into the picture, this, too, is a mutual sharing in contrast to the oftentimes egocentric lovemaking behavior of the virile 20-year-old male.

Sex appeal does continue to appear among the top desirable qualities in a female; however, men in their thirties no longer equate sex appeal with breast size, terrific bodies, gorgeous features, etc. Rather, they talk generally about a number of characteristics that all add up to sex appeal. These include personality as well as body type.

This shift in focus doesn't mean that once a woman enters the thirties decade she can discount or minimize the need to be sexually appealing. The sexual component to a relationship is still central in the thirties just as it is in the twenties, forties, fifties, and beyond.

What does change from the twenties to the thirties is the expression of the sexual appeal. Women in their twenties can be blatant about it. If they wear a bikini, the skimpier the better impression it makes. The way a woman walks can be sexually provocative to males in their twenties; they're not interested in subtle maneuvers. The sexual dance must be strong, vivid, and explicit. In fact, if a woman doesn't spell out her sex appeal in detail for the man in his twenties, he may be oblivious to it.

The male in his thirties, however, is more complex. A little subtlety goes a long way. The thirties woman doesn't have to flaunt her sexuality in the same way a woman in her twenties might if she wants to attract her ideal. The promise, the suggestion, the mystery are going to work wonders for a man in his thirties. He, like the woman of that age, enjoys candelight and conversation.

The male in his twenties doesn't mind bright neon lights in diners and lots of noise. The male in his thirties prefers a quiet restaurant, shadows, subdued tones. His ears are more sensitive. The blaring music he might have rocked to when he was 20 now strikes him as noisy and discordant. Everything has to be softer and more toned down. A revealing dress isn't always the one that will send him into paroxysms of pleasure. It might even annoy him.

Kim, 33, said that she was stunned when Kenneth, the man she had been dating for some time, made a remark about a dress she was wearing. "This is a guy I've been having sex with for three months. We're hardly strangers to each other. I thought I'd get this sexy dress for a big affair we were going to. It wasn't all that suggestive—a bit lower cut than what I usually wear. I thought it was kind of nice and I walked out of the bedroom and he asked me if I didn't have anything else to wear. Two hundred dollars plus tax, and he asks me if I didn't have anything else to wear. He said the one I had on was 'much too revealing.' Much too revealing! This is the guy who when we were together doesn't like clothes on me or him. I mean he has *no* hangups, believe me."

There was a major argument. Kim was in tears. Her boy friend was mute. They were going to call the evening off. Finally, there was a sullen compromise. Kim put on an evening sweater.

"The evening was ruined. We barely talked to each

other. I just thought it horrible of him to put me down and make me feel cheap."

Contrary to what it might seem, Kenneth hadn't changed overnight into a prude. Then what happened? The answer is that Kenneth is in his thirties instead of his twenties. If he were 23 instead of 33 and Kim walked out in a revealing gown, he would have whistled, enjoyed the reactions of his friends, and even joked about suggestive comments they might have made about her sexiness. After all, there's nothing like the evaluation of peers to convince a man that he's a powerful, potent male.

With his increased age, Kenneth still wants to be seen as a powerful, potent male but he prefers that his ideal reserve most of that aspect of herself for a private showing. The suggestion of sex is fine. After all, if he's going to prove he's macho to his buddies, his girl friend shouldn't be wearing a shapeless cover-up. However, what he doesn't enjoy is someone who belongs to him deliberately exposing herself to the world.

By no means are his sexual desires or ability to perform waning. If anything, one of the problems faced by busy men and women in their thirties is to find time for sex. Weeknights they're both at the office late. Friday nights, couples go out to dine and come home exhausted. Fatigue and an extra glass of wine send them off to dreamland. Saturday nights, a movie after a day of shopping, doesn't allow much time for a lot of foreplay or sex.

The situation can become compounded when the young couples in their thirties are both working, and there are young children around. Sex takes time, leisure, a relaxed mood. Sex also takes energy. Those in their twenties, who aren't encumbered with too many concerns about jobs and family responsibilities, have the energy, bounce, and time to have all the sexual delights they can manage. For the busy thirties, involved in their careers, sex sometimes becomes something one has to squeeze in between luncheon engagements, office meetings, and other appointments. Sex in the thirties, although wanted and needed, sometimes begins to backslide, and thus the first seeds of marital discord are sown.

THIRTIES CAN LISTEN AND CAN REACT

Males in their thirties can listen, do listen, and want to listen. They're not only concerned with finding out who they are in relationship to the world, but they want to check out their thinking with someone else. They can listen and they can react. This comes as a surprise to some women who have just about given up on men after the egoism of the monologues of the twenties.

Neil, 34, commented: "I can't take a plastic woman sitting opposite me at the dinner table. She's got to be more than a face and a figure. I want someone who knows her own mind, who isn't a rubber stamp agreeing with whatever I say. I think an ideal woman should have ideas of her own. I want to feel I can trust her opinions. I guess what I'm saying is I want the perfect friend in the opposite sex."

Dates in the thirties, for example, include a lot more sitting and talking in restaurants than couples in their twenties would ever dream of doing. Marrieds in their thirties consider a great evening one that might just be a lengthy conversation in the living room, with him sprawled on the floor, her head in his lap. Talk, talk, and more talk is great for the thirties decade, according to both men and women.

The need for sharing is very intense and real during

Thirties / The Status Decade 79

this decade. In fact, single men in their thirties suddenly become very much interested in settling down. They begin to talk about being tired of the singles' scene. One-night-stands no longer please them. In fact, that kind of behavior seems childish.

"I guess I'm feeling my age," said Don. "I can't run around looking for someone. I don't want to do that, I don't even raise hell when my mom says she has a great person to fix me up with. That's how far along I've come."

Don hasn't settled on any one woman yet. However, now that he has a foot in the door of a company and can see his future laid out in front of him with advancements, promotions, and salary increases, he would like to share it all with someone. For the first time Don's married friends arouse his envy.

"THERE'S GOT TO BE REAL UNDERSTANDING BETWEEN US"

The top characteristics for ninety percent of the women in their thirties were intimacy, empathy, sensitivity, romance, warmth, love, and caring. And when these traits were gone into in depth during in-person interviews, it was apparent that there was a strong practical reason for their importance. Thirty-five-year-old Tammy said of her ideal husband: "We both work. We're pretty tired some nights. We've got the kids to deal with, the house. There has to be real understanding between us. We've got to know that if we're snappish the other person can't take it personally. If we did, we'd have been divorced ten times over. Some nights we don't feel like talking until we get the kids settled and sit down to dinner. Not every day is that bad, of course."

For women in their thirties intimacy with a spouse was

frequently tied to the everyday routines of living. Patty, 37, said: "Being intimate, and that's what a marriage is all about, means a husband will grab the vacuum on Saturday morning if he knows you're on edge without you having to tell him. He'll take a day off from work if the kids are sick. Both of you will be on the same wavelength. He'll know how you feel and you'll know how he feels without having to explain all the time."

Another dimension that showed up in the thirties that, by and large, seldom appeared in the twenties were references to practical attributes. Some seventy-five percent of the women in their thirties rated hard-worker, responsibility, good provider, financial security, appreciative of wife's working and earning power, among the top choices of ideal traits.

Tess, 35, commented: "My husband is proud of me. He brags about my job. An ideal man is one who takes his work seriously and feels the same way about his wife's job."

Nina, 33, recently broke up with a man whom she had been living with for the past four years. "If we married, he would expect me to stay home, raise a family, and take care of him. He wanted a glorified housekeeper. He isn't my ideal for sure though I still admire lots of his qualities."

Women in their thirties haven't forgotten about love or romance, even though sometimes these two qualities come off as second best to being a good provider. Edwina, 36, had this to say about romance: "There isn't all that much time for hand holding with four kids underfoot. Right now I'll take more helping out with the laundry than romance."

Other women agreed with Betty, 37, who said: "When I was young I suppose romance was sitting in the back of a car or in the balcony of a movie theatre. I think about a romantic intimate relationship differently now. It's more sharing. Like my husband and I will go over things together. I can count on him; he can count on me. It's a closeness—a friend with romance."

Many women, however, were definitely not content to let romance be so tinged with practicality. Jill, 34, said: "I'd feel awful if my husband didn't send me a valentine. I don't care how corny it is for some people. It's not for me. I want him to remember my birthday, our anniversary. I like it when he brings me flowers, even when there isn't a holiday. When romance goes out of marriage, that marriage is dead."

A number of the women in their thirties also mention as an ideal trait a man who is secure in his masculinity. Women in their twenties see their ideals as "he men", flexing muscles, sporting broad shoulders, enjoying sports. When women in their thirties mention ideal men as being secure in their masculinity, they are thinking about men who can share family responsibilities that are not typically thought of as part of a male role. "If a guy is secure about who he is," said Rita, 35, "he won't feel it is a big deal because he gives a baby a bottle or changes diapers. A man who is so hung up on his macho image can't do these things."

Although the women were asked to describe their ideals in terms of positive traits, one group in their thirties, all of them divorced, said they thought about an ideal man many times in terms of traits they did not want as well as traits they considered desirable. "I was burned once," said Josephine, 34, mother of one child. "In thinking about an ideal I have to think about what turned me off the first time. This time I want a man who doesn't go out all the time. My former husband was out with the boys every night. I don't care about a lot of things, but for sure I want a guy who thinks of home as a place where the family is, not just a bed to sleep in."

RECIPROCAL REACTIONS IN THE 30'S

For the couple in their thirties, the sexual intensity of the twenties is somewhat reduced, and other concerns and needs come to the fore. The husband is primarily concerned with generating a career, and also with raising a family and establishing a place in society. Although the wife shares many of the same concerns as her husband, her priorities are likely to be somewhat different. In her day-to-day life, the steady demands of family and home are usually central, and at the same time, with rapidly increasing frequency these days, she carries responsibilities for work outside the home.

Faced with the challenges of establishing and building his career, the husband in his thirties needs the psychological support of his wife. In one form or another, he needs to hear from his wife the loud and clear message: "I have faith in you, in your abilities, your talents, your energy, your capacity to achieve the goals you have set." And the wife, in addition to her husband's practical support in carrying out the endless round of daily tasks, needs to hear from her husband the message: "I respect and value all you do in your multiple roles of mother, wife, and worker."

This is without a doubt a decade of heavy and seemingly unceasing demands as husband and wife generate careers, a family, and a way of life together. The mutual, reciprocal support they provide each other is especially crucial during this developmental stage.

THE FORTIES

The Age of Reassurance

"I WANT A WOMAN WHO UNDERSTANDS ME"

"I want out. I'm tired of my marriage, tired of the rut. Lately, I've thought a lot about getting a divorce. I want a woman who understands me, who appreciates me. I need someone who wants what I do—to have fun in life. I don't give a damn if the bathroom ever gets painted. I want a woman who arouses my sexual desires. That's not my wife. With her, sex goes on a schedule along with the rest of her business appointments."

The rumblings of unrest, characteristic of the forties, have suddenly entered James' consciousness. In his thirties, he was filled with admiration for his wife's capabilities. Somehow she managed the many roles of wife, mother, electrician, chauffeur, social chairman, and businesswoman with charm and ease. Suddenly, with an almost overnight abruptness, these once highly prized virtues seem unimportant to him.

doubt it's that sudden

Beatrice was justifiably stunned by his reactions when James told her that it didn't matter if she worked eight to six, prepared dinner, resurfaced the driveway, repaired broken screens, entertained his business associates, and brought home a good paycheck because she turned him off in bed. She wasn't the sexual charmer he wanted and needed.

James' sudden change in priorities is by no means an unusual one. An overwhelming majority of forties men, married, divorced or still single, list such terms as sexy, good body, great in bed, a good figure, someone who is a sexy playmate as top traits of an ideal woman.

The strong emphasis on sex and sexual pleasures has been pretty much missing for a decade. Men in their forties care far less about companionship and friendship than do men in their thirties. In spirit, they revert right back to the twenties with their preoccupation with sex.

Martin, 44, commented: "Good-looking women attract my attention. I'm like every other red-blooded guy. I don't have to get into bed with every woman who arouses me, though that isn't such a bad idea. But let's face it. A good looking sexy woman comes into the room, and I think about what it would be like to go to bed with her. Maybe I think more about this now because of my wife. She's put on quite a few pounds; she doesn't turn me on. More times than not I hear 'I'm tired' from her. I bet this happens to a lot of guys. No mystery why my mind wanders."

Martin may ascribe some of his problems to his wife. But his increased interest in sex and desires for new sexual experiences are also due to a concern about his own middle age. It's often not easy for men or women to realize they are growing older and looking a little grayer, a bit less

Forties / The Age of Reassurance

youthful. They realize they're becoming the older generation.

For men this concern about aging frequently centers around the ability to perform sexually. What really bothers them is the fear of impotence. Chances are, a man in his forties has a tiring job and works long hours. He may question his own achievements and realize for the first time that he hasn't quite made the mark he hoped he would make in the dreaming and excitement of his twenties and thirties. Fatigue, tension, a few aches and pains that were never there before, a new level of sensitivity about his thinning hair—all threaten his self image. Aging signs cut into his consciousness like a sharp knife and make him fearful that he can't achieve and maintain an erection.

Sean, 44, has been visiting a sex therapist. In the past he always enjoyed sex and never had any problems. Now he finds it almost burdensome. Not only is he less interested in sex but he is also unable to sustain an erection: "My sexual drive is zilch."

Fears about decreased sexual drive often make a 40-plus-year-old man frantic. Nothing worries him more than the threat of impotency, the fear of losing his masculinity. When his penis fails to erect and remain erected, he becomes depressed and, if he's married, his typical recourse is to blame his wife.

Lewis, 45, said: "Sure I think about an ideal woman who wears a sexy negligee and looks like she wanted to get into bed rather than someone like my wife who wears flannel nightgowns and asks me, 'Honey, can we have sex later? I've got to get a few more loads of laundry done.' Or she turns over and tells me, 'It's been a long day at the office and I'm dead tired. How about the morning?'

Is there something wrong with me because I'd like to be with a woman who turns me on? I've had enough of the old routine. There's no surprise, no mystery, nothing I don't know. Our sex life is like a broken record we keep trying to play."

No wonder then that many 40-plus-year-old men, who have been plagued with flacid penises, talk about ideal women as having big bosoms and rounded bottoms. Their ideals are naked playmates in bed who are exciting and excited by males in their forties. It's this male who often pinches backsides in offices, has tête-à-têtes at the water cooler, and stops for a drink and a bit of dalliance perhaps after work. The sexual act or the possibility of sexual consummation reaffirms to a male in his forties that once again he has the verve and vigor he remembers having in his early twenties when his goal was to score with as many women as possible.

Patrick, 44, described his ideal woman as about 25, give or take a few years. "I don't want any of the flat-chested types who look like boys. She has to have a gorgeous figure and a face to match."

More important than the specifics about her height and weight and curves is the ability this phantom mistress has to turn Patrick on. Seeing her would be enough to get him aroused. When he thinks of an ideal woman, he doesn't see her wearing an apron and standing in front of a kitchen stove, nor does he think about how well she handles a word processor or a computer. What he does think about, however, is how well she moves in bed, in the back of a car, or any place that sex might take place.

When males in their forties were asked to draw their ideal women and put in as many details as possible, they had no problems filling in anatomical specifics, often exag-

Forties / The Age of Reassurance

gerating certain parts of the body, such as breasts and nipples way out of proportion to the rest of the body.

Sexual activity and attractiveness, whether it is the ability to arouse a man, performance in bed, or willingness to try new techniques, consistently appear among the most important characteristics mentioned by men in their forties.

WHY THIS FOCUS ON SEX?

It comes as a shock for many women of the same age bracket to suddenly confront this almost single-minded interest and concern with sexual matters.

Freud might have described the behavior as a temporary regression to a state of polymorphous perverse sexuality. When he thinks in such wild romantic terms about this stunning female who will capture him, welcome him with open arms and open vagina to assert his maleness he's merely responding to his own biology. It's a fact that a major part of a man's identity is his maleness and he needs to affirm to himself that he is a male. His style and his desires are not pathological or amoral. They're necessary, fundamental, and intrinsic to his identity.

In order to understand why men of this age concentrate on sexual traits in women we really have to consider their whole psycho-social development. They are worried about performance. They worry about how well they are doing in their jobs, in their careers. Suddenly at this juncture in life there is an awareness that they are middle-aged, and there are again questions about the direction their lives are taking. There is a natural and inevitable slowing down. A 40-year-old man can be muscular, vigorous, physically fit, but when he compares himself to a 20-year-old he realizes, with an almost rude awakening, that he is older. He's not 20 nor is he 30, nor is he 35. He's getting on in years, and he can't smash the tennis ball around the court the way he did when he was young.

He's aware of the power and potency of younger men, whether it be on a playing field, or in an office. Performance of *any* sort is on his mind and sexual performance is just one of many performances he worries about. When he thinks about "performance" with an ideal, he doesn't think about how well he can interest her in a stock merger, he thinks of "performance" in terms of sex. This simply means that an ideal has to arouse him quickly, efficiently and with great ease. This also means that his erection culminates in ejaculation. Once this happens, the male in his forties can breathe a welcome sigh of relief. He's reassured himself that he's a potent, powerful male animal to be reckoned with. He succeeded in his youth. He managed sex in his thirties, and "By God," he's still performing with consummate ease and skill in his forties.

Concern about his virility continues throughout the decade. When he worries about his potency, he becomes frantic. This means he can't perform. He worries more, and he's finally caught in a vicious cycle. No wonder his fantasies include bigger and bigger breasts and backsides, more and more sexual gyrations. What he's trying to do with his sexual fantasies is to make sure that he can erect his penis and prove his maleness to himself. No matter how many times the act takes place successfully, the need for confirmation of potency doesn't diminish. It isn't that he can have a one-shot fantasy, have sex, and thus end his concern. The fantasy goes on and the necessity to repeat the confirmation continues unabated.

"I THINK HE'S ACTING LIKE A BIG KID"

The wife of a man in his forties often has to bear the brunt of her husband's sexual fears. His self-doubts lead him to blame her. This makes psychological sense. After all, if he's having trouble with his sexual behavior he certainly isn't going to blame himself. A wife is a convenient and easy target.

William, 44, who faced a temporary setback in sexual performance with less than enthusiasm, said: "There's no question in my mind that the fault is with my wife." William accuses her of having lost interest in sex. "I blame her for not trying to make herself attractive. We have to have sex on her terms."

As an example, he cited coming home from work early one day thinking about sex. "It was a warm spring day. I drove into the driveway of the house and she runs out, 'What's wrong?' I told her nothing was wrong. When I suggested sex you would have thought I was some sort of perverted rapist. 'In the afternoon?' she asks me. 'Yeah,' I told her, 'the afternoon. What's wrong with the afternoon?' She said she was planning to go to the store. I said, 'The hell with the store.' 'Tonight,' she tells me. 'Tonight is five hours off.' I felt like reminding her it wasn't too long ago when it didn't matter where or when with her. Now suddenly it has to be at night, with the door closed, and the shades down. I told her, 'We're big people.' She made me feel like I was some damn adolescent. By the time I got into the house I was turned off."

For William, his wife's lack of enthusiasm for sex in the middle of the day was an example of why it was her fault that his sexual powers were on the decline. In fact, her rejection was a stab at his virility. Therefore, it is no surprise that he accuses her of being old, frigid, narrow-minded, and, of course, insensitive.

Thus when William settles back into a comfortable chair and closes his eyes, it makes sense that the image floating in his imagination is a woman scantily clad, beautifully built, enticing him with a winning smile and a crook of a supple finger into bed. It is the image of someone who wants him sexually and this alone is the impetus he needs to arouse him and enable him to perform. At times like these, despite the extra couple of pounds he has put on and his thinning hair, he feels as jaunty and excitingly male as he felt two decades ago.

Women in their forties frequently react with surprise at their husbands' resurgence of strong sexual desires. Nora, 44, said: "I can't understand what's gotten into him at his age. It's either feast or famine. I think he's acting like a big kid. He bought me this ridiculous sexy nightgown. I had to take it back. I mean, really, it was the kind of gown a 20-year-old would wear. I love good clothes. He knows that, but I don't want to look like some streetwalker even if it is just in my own bedroom. It just was so wrong. But it isn't the gown that bothers me. It's this sexiness. He really is ridiculous at times. It's embarrassing me no end, the game playing he wants to get into. I would have thought all that was done and finished with after adolescence."

"HE DOESN'T HAVE TO BE HANDSOME"

For women in this age group, sexual references of any sort are intensely personal. When women, for example, talk with other women they usually do not discuss their sexual exploits. This simply isn't done. Women did cite physical attributes as being important but only in the sense that they wanted their ideals to be attractive and of pleasing appearance. "He doesn't have to be handsome," said Carol, 44. "I do like a man who has a nice build, well, what I mean is a man who's not sloppy-looking or grossly overweight."

In describing their ideal men, not one single woman in her forties praised or mentioned the size of a man's penis, or the curve of his buttocks. Specific attributes of a male's genitals simply were ignored. In talking about ideals and sex, most of the women are evasive and speak in euphemisms.

Beth, 45, said: "Sex is part of life. Under the right conditions, at the right time of day, it's a very meaningful relationship." Implicit in her statements about sex was the notion of "rightness." For sex to work, the situation had to be right; the timing had to be right; she had to feel right. She admitted that sexual desire didn't just come on impulsively the way it seemed to for her mid-forties husband.

"He'll come home after a hard day at the office. He'll even have a stack of work he has to do in the evening. The kids will be driving him batty with questions and demands. But he can get into bed and he'll want sex. He seems to turn on his desires at the drop of a hat."

Beth said it wasn't the same with her: "I can't just get turned on like that. The things I have to do often intrude on my thoughts. We'll have sex and right afterwards I'll remember I have to make an appointment with the orthodontist. Our daughter is getting braces and I was supposed to make an appointment. I can't snap my fingers and get rid of all the thoughts going on in my head. I can't just shut the door and pop into bed. I need a winding down, a leading into sex."

Women in their forties are out in the world working or, if not working, active in countless projects and activities outside the home. They have many more roles than those of wife and mother. Whitney, a 44-year-old mother of two, said: "I've gone back to school. I work part time. I've got the house and kids to take care of. I could use a computer for a brain."

Getting chores accomplished, completing the long list of things to do which she has in her mental calendar often make sex something that has to be squeezed into a schedule. An ideal man for the busy 40's woman would be someone who takes responsibility for seeing that the dishwasher detergent doesn't run out, for fixing the screen door—someone who would help with the shopping and cooking, and chauffeuring. Life is so busy and full that, if one is not careful, sex can become a burden—one more task on a busy, exhausting list.

"It would be great," said Virginia, 48, "if I was married to an ideal man who could satisfy me sexually. Sex was fun in my twenties. I thought it would go on that way. But there was a long stretch of time when sex took a back seat. Kids, the demands of being a mom full time, a house to take care of, took all my energies. Now I've gone through menopause.

"The kids are away at college. I don't worry about locked doors. I don't have to shout, 'Don't come in. Mommy and daddy are sleeping.' What stories parents make up. I mean I'm yelling, 'I'm sleeping.' I often wonder about the kids outside the door trying to listen. Kids suspect an awful lot, especially when that bedroom door is closed in the middle of the afternoon. And now that it doesn't matter when or how, my husband is the one who is tired. He's the one who rolls over and goes to sleep. It really bothers me. I've had the experience of multiple orgasms the first time in my life. They're fantastic. I have to admit I'm sorry now I didn't discover them long before this. It kills me to think of all the fun I've missed. I'm ready to make up for lost time."

Virginia is not alone. Many women in their forties consider their increased sexual vigor to be a consequence of menopause, the loosening up of family demands, the enjoyment they are having working, and the fact that kids aren't taking up all their free time. This group of women want active sexual partners who satisfy their needs. The problem is how to communicate this desire.

"I think that's where the split comes," said Marge, a 47-year-old woman who was recently divorced. "My husband's eyes turned elsewhere. He started dating women at the office—the young pubescent types. I told him he was right out of a mid-life crisis book. It's not that I didn't want sex, didn't want to be the active sexual partner he needed. I just didn't know how to go about it. I think women in their late 40's feel awkward about letting men know they have strong sexual needs.

"I, myself, have made disparaging remarks about older women who show an active interest in sex—you know, act seductive with men. Women like that are food for gossip. I think most women are taught that it's not nice. Older women should hide their sexual desires. Young women today won't have this problem when they're my age. They're growing up differently."

There is no question that discussion of sexual pleasures and sexual ideals are sensitive subjects for women past 40. As we grow older in our culture, admission of sexual delights and indulgences become more and more forbidden topics. Every now and then there are "startling" surveys showing that older people enjoy sex. The results are always considered revelations. It's very much like "the emperor has no clothes on." Older people always knew sex was fun, but after 40 you don't talk much about it, and particularly if you're over 40 and female.

"HE'LL PUT HIS ARMS AROUND ME AND SAY I LOVE YOU"

What counts most with women in their forties in terms of an ideal mate? Notwithstanding individual differences, there is one thread that runs through all the women's descriptions of an ideal man. That man must have the capacity for intimacy. He can be fat or he can be skinny; he can be tall or he can be short; he can have lots of wavy hair or no hair. He can come in all shapes and sizes; he can bear about as much resemblance to Tom Sellack, Robert Redford, or Paul Newman as a lion does to an ostrich. However, to fulfill a woman's concept of an ideal at this age, a man must have a capacity for intimacy and romance.

The definition of intimacy for women in their forties differs in a number of ways from women in the other age groups. Like those in their twenties and thirties, women in their forties want to be able to communicate and to be understood but in addition, as a consequence of their age, they need the overt, explicit, and clear-cut messages about how desirable they are.

Francine, 46, said: "I think needs of women in their forties are different because we're so much on the giving end. We give love to the kids. We're the ones giving love to our busy husbands. Suddenly there's a little voice inside of you crying, 'What about me?'"

"An ideal man," said Geraldine, "will tell me how attractive he finds me. He'll put his arms around me. We'll curl up in bed next to each other. The warmth of his body will beat an electric blanket any night. I'll feel relaxed, soothed. All the worries and aggravation of the day will fade. He'll tell me he loves me as much now as when we got married, and he won't mind if the kids are around listening to him say this. It may be flattery, but I tell him 'Keep it coming.' He remembers my birthday, our anniversary. I don't have to remind him a dozen times. That's what an ideal spouse does."

Louise, 47, is divorced. She said she didn't miss intercourse, but she did miss a man's intimate attentions. "I miss touching. I miss the way my former husband was when we were first married. The feeling of being wanted. When I go out with men now it's hard to get them to understand that I don't feel sex-starved, I feel love-starved, romance-starved, intimate-starved."

WOMEN SOMETIMES RUN SCARED

Why might women in their forties have this craving to be told they're still attractive, still desirable? Why the special fears of this decade? Part of the problem is that many women in this age are running a bit scared. They are concerned about their sexual appeal. They are aware of aging signs, graying hair, wrinkles, dry skin, and very much want to hear they're still desirable and attractive.

Many 40-plus women agree with Sylvia, 45, who said: "Hearing I'm still attractive does more for my ego than all the new dresses in the world. When I was younger and was told this, I knew it was true. When you're my age, all you have are doubts. You need to hear nice things said. It can make my day at work. Just hearing it makes me feel good. It's not narcissistic. I'm just an average, middle-aged woman who doesn't want the world or her ideal man to put her on a back shelf."

Given the wandering eyes of some males in their forties, and the worries women in that age group have about their physical attractiveness and sex appeal, it probably is no surprise that references to monogamy suddenly appear among the top choices of characteristics. Women in their twenties and thirties rarely refer to monogamy as an ideal trait. Many young women assume a marriage goes on forever. Middle-aged women are more realistic.

Sally, 40, comments: "We have only two couples left intact from a whole crowd that used to live in the same building when we were all first married. Us and one other. My friend and I look at each other and wonder if we're next on a divorce list. Marriages we thought would never break up end in court. And these are marriages that seemed to be going strong for more than fifteen years—a lot even longer. It's enough to make even someone as secure as myself scared. You're so right if you say I feel vulnerable. I watch middle-aged men buying fancy clothing, tight pants, getting their hair styled, and the next thing I hear he's in to see a lawyer and walking out of the courthouse with some chick holding on to his arm." Many women in their forties share Sally's feelings and concern. And thus, traits such as loyalty, commitment, and monogamous behavior are often mentioned as traits of an ideal spouse.

Helene, 47, explains that by monogamy she doesn't only mean one legal wife. "An ideal spouse for me is monogamous in thoughts, feelings, as well as behavior. Years ago, divorce among older couples was unheard of. I mean, none of my mother's friends ended marriages just about the time they were going to become grandparents. And I hear

Forties / The Age of Reassurance

about that happening today. The man next door to us left his wife. We all knew they had a few problems. Years ago couples would have hung in there. The storm would have passed. They would have stayed together. People don't have to nowadays. Divorce is a lot easier, so couples give up and get out no matter their ages."

Many women in their forties feel that breakup among middle-aged couples can be attributed to the inability of males of the same age group to grow old gracefully. In fact, men's refusal to accept the aging process is frequently mentioned by women approaching the end of this decade.

Lillian, 48, noted: "My ideal is not going to be upset by his gray hair. He'll think of the two of us as romantic as ever. This means we don't have to be sprawled out in the back of a car like teenagers."

For women in their forties romantic monogamy is sedate and controlled, soft and warm, more like being under a down comforter on a snowy evening than skipping naked across a sandy beach.

THE GIVE AND TAKE OF A RELATIONSHIP

Women in this age group also value give and take in a relationship. "It's so important," said Moira, 46, "that my husband doesn't dig his heels in and is so dead sure he's always right. For me that trait means everything. I don't want that smug attitude. I think it's better if a man has some perspective on himself, can laugh at himself as well as with himself." Thus, women in their forties often rate a sense of humor as an important trait. They want to laugh about some of life's problems, some of life's bumps.

In contrast, a sense of humor, and the ability to laugh at oneself are rarely priorities as far as 40's men are concerned. In interviews, a few did mention a sense of humor. However, the contrast between men and women in their forties in this respect is astonishing. In a way, it is a contradiction of sorts. The men want fun and good times. The women tend to be much more serious than the men, and yet they mention a sense of humor as a trait they esteem in an ideal. Perhaps it is precisely because they take life more seriously that humor becomes so important to women in their forties. And perhaps men in this age bracket don't mention humor simply because they don't consider a sense of humor as a category apart from the capacity to have a good time.

"LET'S DO SOMETHING CRAZY AND WILD"

The descriptions of ideal women given by men in their 40's are clearly influenced by their need for change and their longing to experience excitement and adventure.

Dan, 47, noted: "I want change in my life. I made good in my business. And I'd like to try something new. I want to give it all up but my wife is scared. She likes the way we live now. She's settled and I want adventure. You don't get a chance for a second time around in life. Let's do something crazy and wild, I tell her. I don't want to sit here waiting for a pension and Social Security."

He wanted his wife to share his high spirits, excitement, and eagerness to break with the patterns of work and demands of family obligations. This quest for newness, change, and adventure left some women we interviewed with the impression that their husbands had gone crazy: "He wanted to buy a motorcycle at his age!" one explained. There are better things to do with his time and our money."

Men in their forties are often concerned with breaking out of the ruts of daily life they have established over the previous two decades. They are engaged in the process of reexamining their lives and themselves, and in this process they may fantasize about radical shifts in life style. They dream about change and adventure, and it is little wonder, then, that their descriptions of an ideal woman reflect their hunger for excitement.

"HE DOESN'T WANT TO LISTEN"

Women in all the age groups placed a high premium on a man's ability to listen and communicate, but women in their forties placed a special emphasis on communication skills. Grete, 47, commented about her husband: "I'm desperate to talk to him, to find out what is going wrong, to break the deadlock. But he's closed down. He doesn't want to listen. He won't even fight with me anymore. We don't argue. There's just this deadly silence between the two of us."

Men in this age bracket rarely talk about communication skills. In fact, when the topic was brought up some men drew a blank. Steven, 45, said: "Communication is a bunch of bullshit. What are you supposed to do after 40, learn to talk? I mean, come on now. If you have to start developing skills like that at my age, something is wrong."

The art of talking and the art of listening, he felt, were not arts that pertained to marriage, but to the workplace. Jonathan, an advertising executive in his mid-forties, admits to having attended seminars to improve his communication skills, ability to persuade people, to listen, and to evaluate, but the last thing he would think of is associating these skills with a marriage or with the woman he's dating now that he's divorced. "You talk, that's it. One talks, then the other. You don't sit and chew over who's talking about what. I mean, my God, this sounds like turning a romantic relationship into some kind of business deal."

There's no doubt that communication skills, extra measures of sensitivity, romantic behavior, commitment to marriage and monogamy, and single-minded devotion to another are all things men value in an ideal spouse. But they do not scrutinize or think about these characteristics in the same concrete way that women do. Certainly many men value monogamy and are as distraught as a woman would be if they discover wives or girl friends cheating on them. Similarly, they want to talk to their ideals, and enjoy being listened to. But most men take these traits for granted. They are either present in a relationship or they are not. Most 40's men felt it was mindless to sit down and engage in self-analysis before embarking on a relationship or continuing with one.

GENTLE AND ADVENTUROUS, CALM AND HIGH-SPIRITED

And finally, as we analyzed the data, an intriguing contradiction emerged. Sixty-five percent of the men who mention high spirits, adventuresome, sexy, appealing physically, fun loving, and dashing as important traits also emphasize calmness, gentleness, charming, affectionate, among the top qualities of an ideal woman. In view of the male's reawakening of youthful dreams, and desires to cut loose from conventions, their citing these traits was puzzling.

However, such contradictions are inherent in the psychosocial dynamics of male in his forties. At the same time

Forties / The Age of Reassurance

he wants to cut loose, he wants to retain the warmth and safety of marriage. Perhaps his emphasis on words such as calm, poised, gentle, generous, forgiving suggest that, on the one hand, the male is ready to burst forth and, on the other hand, he welcomes the safety net his present life affords him.

RECIPROCAL REACTIONS IN THE FORTIES

Psychological development in the forties imposes special stresses on marital relationships at this stage, and the importance of reciprocal supportive reactions cannot be overemphasized.

The husband needs his wife's tolerance and acceptance of his emotional ups and downs in his trial-and-error efforts at redefining his adult identity. In turn, the wife needs her husband's explicit reassurance of her desirability and self-worth, and his encouragement to expand her range of interests and activities, to explore and realize her potential and fulfill herself in ways that have been blocked by the multitude of responsibilities she has carried during the previous decade.

For many couples, this is an emotionally bumpy period as both husband and wife reexamine and reestablish their psychological identities. It is a period during which it is all too easy to blame one's spouse for the frustrations and stresses that are, in fact, common and normal at this stage of adult development. It is also a period in which the reciprocal support of husband and wife developing in sync can strengthen, more than ever, the bonds of their marriage.

THE FIFTIES
PLUS

Reconciliation

None of the drama, turbulence, restlessness, and confusions of the forties prepares men or women for the glowing incandescence of the fifties and beyond—the golden years in terms of relationships. The changes that occur in descriptions of the ideal spouse, as well as the changes in husbands' and wives' behaviors toward each other, can come as a complete surprise, not only to the fifties themselves, but to their families.

Diane, 26, sums it up: "I still can't believe what's going on with my Dad. It was a nightmare a few years ago. He was at Mom all the time. Mom never said much, but I had an idea Daddy was having an affair with someone at their country club. I couldn't bring myself to ask her what was going on. Sometimes it was terrible going home. I could tell from mom's face that she had been crying. Once in a while she'd fight back. Daddy would storm out of the house. She gave in first—making up.

"I know he wanted a divorce. Mom wouldn't give him one. She hung in there. Now they're like two kids all over again. Daddy brings her flowers. They've started playing golf together. It used to be Daddy would never play with her. Now he insists she go with him. I can't believe what's going on in their lives.

Contrary to what you might assume, Diane's 50-plus-year-old father didn't go for therapy. Nor did her parents see a marriage counselor together. No one helped them out. We aren't detracting from the value of counseling and professional help, but in Diane's parents' case, as many others, the problems were resolved as both spouses moved into the fifties decade.

Jim, a man in his early fifties, described the new feelings he has about himself and life: "I sense a quieting down inside. It's hard to describe—like the old blood pressure isn't racing. I think about my age and I look at the obits and I see people I know and it makes me wonder about my own mortality. You wonder about life. I figure, 'what the hell, life is so short, why make a big deal over something that isn't important.' I try to be selective about what really counts, what really matters."

There may be a last outburst on the part of a fifty-plus year old man, a final storming at his wife as being the source of all his problems, a final slamming of doors, and packing of suitcases, but these storms are more theatrics than serious behavior.

"MY BEST FRIEND"

In many ways the behavior as well as the thinking of a male in his fifties reflects the introspection about personal life and life in general, and these new insights about himself dramatically influence the way he describes an ideal wife. Rather than talk about a woman's body, beauty, and sex appeal, males at this age talk about "best friend."

"I want to enjoy life," said Carl, 54. "There's no one I'd rather enjoy doing things with than my wife."

Carl often calls his wife from work. "I like to talk to her." Oftentimes there is nothing really important on his mind, but he enjoys hearing the sound of her voice.

The notion that an ideal spouse is also a "best friend" is widespread. And along with the "best friend" concept, an interest in communication appears. In the previous decades men seldom referred to communication. If anything, they dismissed the concept as artificial. Men in their fifties are vastly different.

Thomas, 57, notes: "I talk to my wife more than other people. I trust her judgments. I respect what she has to say about people we meet and business deals. She may not know the ins and outs of what I do and for that matter I don't know much about some of the nitty-gritty of her work, but I do consult with her. No question about that."

The concept of an ideal spouse as a companion and best friend shows up right from the start of the decade and continues to become more and more important as the years move on. By the latter half of the fifties, eighty-five percent of the men mention companion, communication, and best friend among the top traits of an ideal spouse.

Not only are these men strong supporters of communication and companionship, but they stress virtues such as sensitivity. They want their ideals to be sensitive to their needs. And what is more striking is that they feel it equally important that they be responsive and sensitive to the needs of their spouses.

GIVE AND TAKE

The egocentrism of a relationship, so common in the early decades, is replaced by a new appreciation and respect for give-and-take, a helping relationship. Men in their thirties might have to have their arms twisted to go to the grocery store, or mop up after a dinner party. Men in their forties are image worriers, so that they can't afford the time or show much interest in sharing the daily chores of life either. However, in the fifties, the companionship that men want in an ideal wife clearly shows how far they are willing to go to establish a fifty-fifty relationship. Men in their fifties and sixties have no qualms about trundling grocery carts, washing dishes after a party, or taking out the vacuum without a hundredth reminding nag from a busy wife.

The need to be companionable extends not only to verbal closeness but to actually being in the presence of an ideal. "I like my wife around," said Arthur, 59. "We don't always have to be talking. Sometimes it's just important that I know she's in the house." For Arthur, an ideal wife is physically present, ready to enter into a conversation, or ready to be silent.

MY IDEAL SHOULD BE PLEASING

What about sex? Sex dominates the thoughts of the twenties. Sex still looms as an important consideration of an ideal spouse in the thirties. In the forties there is a resurgence of the lust that was so much a part of the twenties. Does sexual fantasy disappear in the fifties? Definitely not! However, when it comes to describing an ideal spouse, sexiness, beauty, curves in the right places, all the accoutrements of sex appeal from big bosoms on down are noticeably absent from the fifties' descriptions.

It's not that men in their fifties have become prudes. It's not that erotic behavior or sexy bodies don't awaken their desires. However, when they describe their ideal spouse they simply don't pay much attention to sexual traits. They place far more stress on personality and values.

Frank, 56, comments: "I think, if my wife had a sexy figure, that would be fine. But, that's not what counts in our relationship. Of course, we enjoy sex. But in thinking about her ideal qualities what counts with me is her sensitivity, understanding, warmth, kindness, and generosity."

Men in their fifties are shy about mentioning specific sexual traits or references to physical beauty. In describing the appearance of their ideals, the vast majority agreed with Charles, 58, who said: "My ideal should be pleasing. It's a matter of how she takes care of herself. That's what counts. I like my wife to look her best."

These men's general acceptance of their spouses "as is" might be attributed to their awareness of their own aging bodies. They recognize it may not be fair to criticize a spouse when they, too, have a little more spread around the middle. They, too, feel the pull of gravity which makes their stomach and back muscles collapse at the end of the day. Since they're not always in such marvelous shape themselves, they are rightfully self-conscious about criticizing a spouse or even fantasizing some dream body.

In general, men in their fifties are not hung up on anatomical details, but they clearly take pride in their mates having a nice appearance. Many admitted teasing their spouses about costs of beauty shops, night creams, and clothing bills. But for the men who are happily married, the expenditure on such extras was not resented. A nice appearance added to a relationship but was not a critical factor in a fifties man's evaluation of an ideal.

SWEET AND GENTLE

"It doesn't matter what he looks like," said Therese, 57. "I let my grandchildren worry about looks. My ideal man can have thin hair or no hair. It doesn't concern me at all. But he can't be sloppy. That's my one big condition about how he appears physically. I do not like sloppy men.

"When we go out I want my husband to be dressed nicely. If I didn't say anything he'd go around in an old pair of pants, a baggy jacket. Clothes don't interest him. I insist, when we go out, that he dress up. He does it to please me. What counts with me is his sweetness and gentleness. My husband has a lovely smile. His whole face lights up. He's at ease with himself. Everyone who meets Jack thinks he's self-contained and sweet. For me those are traits that count."

Nearly all of the women in their fifties consider sweetness and gentleness prime qualities of the ideal man. The emphasis these women place on the gentle side of an ideal spouse clearly reflect feelings many women of this age have about themselves. Cora, 58, commented: "The harsh edges seem to be pared away. I notice it in myself. I see it in my friends. I feel softer, a lot more gentle, a lot less pressured. I think it's inevitable in life. You reach a stage where the kids are grown and settled. If they're settled reasonably well, you feel a lot calmer. Of course, you need money to live on, but you don't need the amounts you had to have when there were school bills to pay, kids to support."

Thus the fifties decade marks a time of softening, a time

for drawing into oneself, a change of pace for many people. This does not mean that women in this decade are less involved, less energetic, less concerned people, but it does indicate that they are more self-contained. They often have an inner-directed attitude. Thus when they think about an ideal spouse, they like him to share their relaxed attitude, their serenity, their sense of contentment.

SHARING DOESN'T HAVE TO BE FIFTY-FIFTY

The notion of sharing takes on a special meaning for women in their fifties. They don't think of sharing as a fifty-fifty proposition where "you do the dishes" and "I'll vacuum the floor." Denise, a 56-year-old, notes: "It doesn't matter whether my husband ever does the laundry. Oh, I suppose I cared a lot about this trivia when I was younger. I see my daughter now making a huge fuss because her husband doesn't take the kids to school. Since they both work she feels her time is as important as his. I'm not saying she's wrong. What I am saying is that I don't think about these things with the seriousness I did when I was younger. If he vacuums, he's great; if he doesn't vacuum, well, he's great too. He does other things I don't like to do."

For both the woman and man in their fifties, spending time together is especially important. Mildred, 58, said: "When my husband was younger, he was always working. The family had so little time together. There wasn't time to enjoy life. Now my husband takes time; he makes time. I think that's so important for a family. An ideal man has to care about the family. He has to think about togetherness. He's got to realize that you just can't rush in and out and think that's a relationship."

ONE DAY AT A TIME

As important as sharing is the calmness of men as an ideal trait. "My ideal man is serene and relaxed," said Gwen, 57. "He takes one day at a time. He's not so driven." It is evident that Gwen, like many women in their fifties, values this slowing down of their spouses. "If my husband were still running from one business deal to another, from one activity to another, I don't think I could stand living with him or the pace. It's about time he took time to savor life, to see that what counts is his family, me, the children and grandchildren."

SEX—ONE ASPECT OF TOGETHERNESS

Although women in their fifties rarely describe their ideal spouse in explicitly sexual terms, sex remains an important aspect of the marital relationship. Anna, 59, notes: "I still enjoy sex. It's a part of our relationship but not by any means the main thing. There's so much more to being together—enjoying a walk, for instance. Now if he's too tired to have sex at night I know it's not because he doesn't care; he's tired. This didn't happen years ago. Passion is for the young. I remember sitting in the back of a car, necking—they called it that in my day. If you had asked me then what was my ideal I would have had a lot to say about sex. Now if you asked me would I rather have a sexy man or a healthy, kind, loving one, it would take me about one second to answer. If a man doesn't have his health as you grow older, nothing else matters."

Nearly one hundred percent of the men and women agree with Anna. A healthy ideal was first and foremost in their minds and in second place the fifties-plus group mention fun, a sense of humor, ability to enjoy life. Ideals have to be able to laugh, and to experience life as something to be savored, enjoyed, and cherished in good health.

RECIPROCAL REACTIONS IN THE FIFTIES

After the heavy demands of daily life in the thirties and the developmental turbulence of the forties, the couple in their fifties can capitalize on the psychological strengths they have acquired over the years. Freed from the everyday responsibilities of childcare, no longer concerned with the stresses and challenges of establishing careers, and having resolved the internal turmoil characteristic of the previous decade, the husband and wife can grow even closer than ever before. With fewer external distractions and less internal stress, they can fulfill each other's needs for greater intimacy, mutual sharing, and the deepening enjoyment of their maturity.

Making It Work

Our study incontrovertibly shows that men and women's ideas of a perfect spouse change with age. The ideal spouse of the twenties for either men or women is not always the ideal of the thirties, the forties, or beyond. How does this affect the development of a loving, lasting, in-sync relationship?

Does it mean that a woman in her twenties dons a bikini and swishes around, hips swaying, breasts bouncing? Does she hide all her brains and make sure she listens intently to every word a man in his twenties says?

In her thirties, does she suppress or ignore her own sexual desires, buy a business suit, and earn lots of money while juggling children, a house, mortgages, computers, cars, beauty shop appointments, and so on?

In her forties does she whip off the business suit, take up skydiving and ballooning when she isn't playing polo which hasn't come easily because she's never ridden horses in her life? Does she run out and buy a black lace "teddy" which barely covers her breasts and certainly won't cover most forties' backsides?

In her fifties does she burn the black lace teddy, skip the horseback riding, take off the business suit and take up joint gardening or sharing a golf cart?

Does she have to go through all these gymnastics until the end of the fifties when forever more she can go shoeless if she desires, wear baggy pants and a shirt, unloosen hooks on her bra, turn on the popcorn maker, and settle down in front of the VCR with a nice, sweet, relaxed guy? Could it be that this person who has just come back with her from the grocery store, uncomplainingly vacuumed, taken out the window screens, even washed some of the windows, is the same man who had her jumping fences, and tumbling around in bed at all times of the day just a few short years ago?

Do the results of this study mean that a man in his twenties must suffer the exquisite pain of his "maleness" unsatisfied, hardened and erected in the agony of unfulfillment, while he listens to this gorgeous girl who is the cause of all this agony tell him how she managed to get her word processor hooked up to a master computer system?

Does this study mean that as a man turns 30 he should abandon his career because it absorbs too much of his time and keeps him from meeting the kids after school? Does he cancel his appointments so he can whisk one child off to an orthodontist and go shopping for heavy cream so his wife can make sauce Bernaise for supper? In between all these chores does he also make sure he tells her he adores her and as proof whips out a frilly valentine he spent his *whole* lunch hour making?

Do the findings of this study mean that as a man turns 40 he puts on blinders when he passes the water cooler so that he can't see the young curvaceous woman who has just joined the staff bend over the fountain to get a drink? Does he ignore the extra weight his wife might be putting on and instead say to her, "Darling, I adore twenty pounds more of you in a tight pants suit"?

Does he tell his wife, "I won't buy that flashy sports jacket and the gold chains for my neck. Instead, you take the money and repaper the bathrooms?" Does he make sure that erotic pictures TURN HIM OFF and convince himself that what is really exciting is the new strain of gladioli bulbs that are popping up all over the garden?

Does he pine wistfully for the day when he can shuffle off happily with her to the supermarket and involve himself in a long discussion about which laundry detergent really gets fabrics snow white? Does he reassure himself that he really finds joy in the merry whirl of the vacuum before he can creep into a favorite chair, turn on the VCR and see old childhood movies IF he can stay awake the full two or so hours?

To all of the above questions, our answer is—ABSOLUTELY NOT! Obviously, we've over-simplified some of the central expectations of each decade regarding qualities and characteristics of an ideal spouse. However, the differences between the decades, remain very real.

The division into decades is somewhat arbitrary. Changes do not occur overnight. A man at age 29 doesn't turn 30 and suddenly become a different person with a different concept of a ideal spouse. What may be said however, is that the sequential nature of the changes more or less approximates chronological development. Some people may move along the continuum of changes at a faster rate. Others will go more slowly. The patterns of change, however, are clear and consistent.

The importance of this study for both men and women lies in the recognition that values, goals, needs and attitudes about what constitutes an ideal spouse undergo striking changes over the course of a lifetime. This point can never be minimized or underestimated. It is a critical factor influencing the lasting power of a marriage, and equally important in determining the happiness and contentment of any relationship. The understanding of the direction of the changes is crucial.

Change is very much a part of our culture. We know and expect it in the field of technology. However, we're less comfortable with socio-psychological changes. But no one can afford the luxury of being indifferent to the changing needs and ideals of one's mate. In fact, it is probably more important today than at any other time in our history that attention be paid to the socio-psychological changes of adult life. Because of our fast-paced lives, external pressures, job schedules and so on, people today live more than ever in the demands of the immediate moment. As a consequence, it's very easy to lose sight of what is going on in the life of one's mate.

The happiest couples, the most successful couples, the couples who have marriages that last are those whose normal developmental patterns parallel each other. Difficulties or problems are inevitable when the couples are at different developmental stages and have different concepts about what an ideal spouse should be like. Marital success can be measured by the degree to which couples are living in sync.

* * *

It's sometimes said that "to understand all is to forgive all." This bit of folk wisdom is probably an over-statement; there are undoubtedly instances when all the understanding in the world does not lead to forgiveness. But understanding one another surely makes a significant different in our interpersonal relations.

A wife who sees her 35-year-old husband becoming increasingly concerned with his career, perhaps at the expense of paying less attention to her, may be saved the pangs of jealousy and suspicion if she recognizes that his behavior reflects a normal stage of adult male development. And a husband who sees his 40-year-old wife becoming especially concerned about her appearance and more demanding of his affection may be saved a good deal of worry and perhaps annoyance if he realizes that her behavior is the result of a normal, and temporary, developmental stress. If nothing else, understanding normal developmental changes short-circuits the misperceptions and the misinterpretations that get in the way of living in sync.

CHANGE IS NORMAL AND HEALTHY

Caught up in the demands of day-to-day life, we often lose perspective about ourselves and about those closest to us. With the usual stresses of work, family responsibilities, community activities, and the variety of other obligations that comprise adult life, it is little wonder that we often fail to maintain a calm, long-term perspective on our lives.

As a result, we may not realize that those around us are changing and developing, and that we ourselves are also changing and developing. The changes are often slow and gradual, and we may not recognize that change has occurred until some dramatic event highlights the change. Then, the change may seem so sudden and abrupt that we feel unprepared to deal with it, and we are frustrated, hurt, and unhappy.

There is no absolutely sure way to maintain perspective

on ourselves and others all the time, but it will help if we remind ourselves from time to time that change is normal and healthy in adult life. We are always in the process of developing, and as we develop, our interests, our concerns, and our needs inevitably change. If we can remember this, the changes we sense in ourselves and in others will not seem so surprising or fortuitous. They will make sense to us and thereby be easier to accept and live with.

IT TAKES TIME

In our age of instant coffee, instantaneous worldwide communication, computers that can solve complex problems in seconds, an age when almost everything in our lives seems to be speeded up, we sometimes expect marital problems to be resolved by instant solutions. If they are not, we may assume there must be something "really wrong," and the next step is to see our lawyers for some fast action.

But regardless of how fast we can send rockets to the moon or the speed with which the latest computer can compute, resolving interpersonal problems takes time. There is no instant way to achieve a relationship in sync. Therefore, it is important to give yourselves time.

It's not that time alone will automatically resolve problems between husband and wife, but it takes time to gain mutual understanding and to work out mutually satisfying adaptations.

SPACE TO GROW

As we develop and change over the years, we need opportunities to "try out" our emerging selves in the safety and security of an intimate relationship. We need some "psychological space" in which we can engage in the trial and error behavior that always accompanies psychological development. A marriage with husband and wife in sync provides this safe and secure space.

This means that husband and wife can try out with each other the new roles they are beginning to play in the world, and that they can do so without fear of being critically judged.

Giving each other space to grow and change depends, first, on recognizing that growth and change are normal and natural. But it also depends on both husband and wife appreciating and valuing the continuing development of each other.

DON'T MAKE EMOTIONAL MOUNTAINS OUT OF MOODY MOLEHILLS

Many years ago as first-year graduate students in psychology we "discovered" that our moods and emotional swings had the potential of deep-seated significance. Like all neophytes we became enchanted. Up until that point in our married life we enjoyed our blissful ignorance. If either of us became angry, the other simply walked out of the room until the storm blew over. When one of us was depressed or tense, the other was more than likely to say, "Come on, let's get some ice cream, go to a movie," and that ended the tension. Now, with our new-found knowledge that all behavior is motivated and that sensitivity and analysis should be absolute musts for a successful marital relationship, everything changed. All one of us had to do was to look tense and a barrage of probing questions followed in quick pursuit of the cause. The scenario had a pattern:

"You seem depressed."

"I'm not depressed."
"If you're not depressed, why are you silent?"
"I don't feel like talking."
"That isn't like you. Something happened."
"Nothing happened."
"You might think about your feelings. You did the same thing last week. You're not telling me the truth."

Getting to the bottom of every bit of anger, tension and depression became an obsession.

Although analyzing the emotional ups and downs of one's spouse can be interesting, and sometimes fun, too much analysis is pointless, unnecessary, and potentially dangerous. From time to time everyone experiences moments of tension, anger, and disappointment as well as all the other unhappy emotional states which are an inevitable part of life. Mood changes are perfectly normal. For the most part, these mood swings last a brief time, quickly pass and are forgotten in the current of everyday living. However, if the person we're living with responds to these momentary feelings as if they were a crisis, the mood is less likely to fade away and be forgotten. When the mood feelings become an issue, they lead to other conflicts. Being alert and watchful for every cue of anger, every sign of despair, every bit of nervousness or tension is a full-time watching job. No wonder extrasensitive couples have to get divorced. Day-to-day living is agony. A husband only has to look crooked to get a reaction; the wife only has to complain or be soulful one moment, and that is enough to set off a whole chain reaction.

We are certainly not recommending gross insensitivity; mutual understanding is the undeniable basis of living in sync. But don't overdo a good thing. Don't make emotional mountains out of moody molehills.

SELECTIVE INSENSITIVITY

We recall a discussion with a happily married couple who celebrated their 51st anniversary. He told us that every time they go to a restaurant his wife complains about the cost, service, and the seasoned food, which gives her a stomachache. It doesn't matter where they go or whom they go with, her complaints are invariable. Doesn't he find this habit unbearable, we asked. Wasn't his good time spoiled?

Not at all, was his amused reply. In fact, if we hadn't insisted that he describe some special irritant in his relationship with his wife he probably never would have mentioned this quirk of hers. How did he handle the situation? His solution was quite simple. He didn't really hear her anymore. He had stopped listening to these kinds of complaints. If he hadn't, then he might have become so irritated that they would have ended every social evening with an argument and would have been divorced long ago.

We would not deny that couples should be sensitive and responsive to each other but just as important as sensitivity per se is the tempering of this sensitivity with what we have termed selective insensitivity. Happily married couples have developed and refined this art without even realizing it in most cases. Unhappily married couples seem to take a special delight in making lists of irksome habits.

Kate and Tom have been married for five years. They met during college. Rather than enter marriage without really knowing each other they lived together for two years to see if they were indeed really matched.

"Dating is a lot different from marriage," said Katie. "Even my parents who were against the idea of our living together finally came around to our way. I told them I'd rather I knew about Tom and he knew about me than be surprised by little things after we were married and risk getting a divorce." Living together they both felt would provide them with the opportunity to get to know each other in an intimate situation. Katie felt that her mother hadn't really known her husband so that the continual fighting between the two of them over "silly" things was inevitable. Living with Tom before marriage was insurance against surprises.

For two years they did live together with complete accord. In fact, they only waited the two years because they wanted to make sure they both got jobs in the same city. Five years after the wedding they were desperate for marriage counseling. The relationship had deteriorated.

"Didn't you know during the trial period," we asked Katie, "that Tom's dirty clothes were on the floor of the closet instead of in the laundry basket? Weren't you aware that Tom always acted as if magic would take care of dirty dishes?"

We asked Tom if Katie had all of a sudden developed her habit of talking to friends for hours on the telephone each evening. "Weren't you aware that Katie had a different concept of time, that is, if you agreed to meet at 7 she might show up at 7:30?" We listed each of their complaints trying to determine if any of them had surfaced after the wedding. With few exceptions all the annoyances were present before the marriage. Katie insisted that "it was different."

How was it different? She maintained that when they lived together she didn't pay attention to the small details. After marriage, however, it was different. Tom agreed. Katie had always come late. He had always found this tendency an irritant but in his eagerness to be with her he didn't mind. The marriage license somehow made it legal for them to ignore the fun part of their relationship and zero in on the annoyances.

The annoyances have become a catalyst, starting a whole chain of arguments. For example, Katie now perceives Tom's neglect of doing the dishes as a way of showing her that he is a male chauvinist. Tom feels that Katie's telephone behavior and lateness is a rejection of him as a person. They are searching out profound and deep causes behind their every action. If Tom and Katie continue hard and long enough they will surely wind up another divorce statistic. Perhaps it should be mandatory for every husband and wife who comes up with a negative bit of behavior to also list a positive attribute.

The one and only approach to the petty irritations that crop up inevitably when one is living with someone else is selective insensitivity. It is an unfortunate truism that a great deal of daily life does involve the trivial mechanics of living. There's laundry and shopping, dishes and mowing lawns, bank accounts and telephone bills. Given the range of trivia that consumes one's daily life one can easily see how married couples have a lot to choose from when they concentrate on behavioral differences or habits they find objectionable.

Every couple must set priorities about what is important and what is a potential problem in a relationship. We do not for a moment deny there are some areas where sensitivity is crucial in a relationship. But, more often than not, the complaints of unhappily married couples are issues that demand a healthy dose of selective insensitivity.

KEEP THE LINES OF COMMUNICATION OPEN

Knowing each other's needs depends upon communication. This is surely an obvious fact, but it needs to be stated, and remembered, because it is so central to the process of living in sync. Moreover, one of the most common stumbling blocks to establishing and maintaining a relationship in sync is the failure of husband and wife to keep communication lines open regardless of what has happened.

Sometimes, the breakdown in communication stems from preoccupation with the demands of everyday life—concerns about children, problems at work, financial matters, etc. Involved in the details of daily living, husband and wife may take their relationship for granted and forget the simple fact that communicating with each other about each other and not about the children or the electric bill, is a basic necessity of marriage.

Temporary lapses in communication stemming from preoccupation with day-to-day affairs is not necessarily a serious problem in itself. But it can lead to a serious problem because it may be habit-forming. Without realizing what has happened to them, a couple may avoid talking to each other directly about each other, and thus gradually lose touch with each other's needs and concerns.

An even more serious situation is created by couples who deal with marital problems by withdrawing from each other. Husband or wife may be frustrated, hurt, angry about some issue, and rather than confront the issue directly, withdraw into a psychological shell. This psychological withdrawal may lead, in turn, to the spouse's counter withdrawal, and very soon the couple is communicating with each other only about the most superficial trivia of their lives.

This can only lead to severe frustration and serious marital difficulties. As husband and wife communicate less and less to each other, they inevitably become less aware of each other's feelings and needs, and live in mutual frustration.

Therefore, no matter how painful it may be, regardless of how hurt or angry or confused you might be, keep the lines of communication about each other open because it is only through communication that you can achieve the kind of mutual understanding necessary for living in sync.

IT'S OK TO BE ANGRY

Living in sync doesn't mean that every moment in your marriage will be filled with peaceful, loving joy. No two people can live in perfect synchronization, and there are bound to be times of unrest, dissatisfaction, frustration, and anger. Marital problems don't stem directly from anger itself, but rather from the ways in which couples deal with their anger. It's OK to be angry as long as you remember:

1. *Some frustration and some anger is normal and expected,* even in the most stable of relationships. It doesn't mean that your marriage is bad or that you don't love each other.
2. *Stop playing the blame game,* that common form of marital fighting in which each spouse tries to pin some blame on the other, and both usually end up angrier and more frustrated than before. So, while it is OK to be angry and to express your anger, it's definitely *not* OK to become a prosecutor striving to find your spouse guilty. There is no trick or formula for stopping this hurtful behavior. Just stop it!
3. *Anger communicates information. Pay attention to that information.* Regardless of whether or not you think your

spouse's anger is warranted, anger always conveys a message: "I am frustrated." If you pay attention to this message, rather than to the attacks that may accompany the anger, you are likely to gain fuller understanding of your spouse's needs and thus be able to satisfy these needs more adequately. You may feel that the anger is unwarranted or inappropriate. But regardless of how you feel, try to remember that no matter how illogical the anger may seem to you, it is motivated by some frustration your spouse is experiencing. This motivation is psychologically real for your spouse; pay attention to it. Try to understand it, and use the information to gain a greater understanding of your spouse's feelings.

MIND YOUR MARITAL MANNERS

In every relationship, there are certain implicit rules that guide behavior. These rules are rarely discussed or made explicit in any formal way, but nevertheless most people know the rules, usually follow them, and generally feel more comfortable when the rules are obeyed. There are rules, for example, that guide greetings, rules that guide casual conversations, rules that guide virtually all of our daily social interactions. And indeed, there are rules for marital interactions.

These unspoken rules might be thought of as the manners of marriage. By manners we don't mean the conventions about which fork to use or when to send thank-you notes. Rather, we are referring to those interpersonal behaviors aimed at making the other person feel comfortable and at ease.

Each couple develops a set of marital manners, not by

talking about them, but simply by living together and discovering what behaviors make each other most compatible. There is no general set of marital manners that apply equally to everyone; each couple, on the basis of their own unique experience, gradually evolves a style of marital manners that they find comfortable to live with. Without such manners, life would become chaotic, unpredictable, and in the long-run, unbearable.

Marital manners may cover all aspects of married life, such as rules that guide breakfast conversation, rules that guide sexual relations, rules that guide marital fighting. Most couples, for example, follow some form of a general rule that there is a proper place for marital fights (usually in private), and that there are proper topics to fight about (such as money, in-laws, or disciplining the children) and other topics (tapping especially sensitive areas) that should be avoided even in the heat of battle. Thus, minding their marital manners, a couple can live and love and even fight together with reasonable comfort.

But sometimes, preoccupied with other concerns, manners are forgotten. After all, no husband and wife sit down and explicitly list their mannerly expectations of each other. Marital manners are part of the largely unspoken agreements that husbands and wives have with each other.

At first, forgotten manners might lead only to minor irritations, but minor irritations, if they continue, can grow to major proportions. As a result, a couple may find themselves unable to live in sync, not because of any profound underlying problem, but simply because they have failed to mind the marital manners that ease each other's way in daily living.

Sharing Fun and Pleasure

Discussions about marriage are sometimes carried on in most solemn tones, clearly implying that marriage is business and that there isn't time for fun and pleasure. Yet, this contradicts an essential ingredient of living in sync, for regardless of what else they do, husbands and wives who are living in sync enjoy each other, have fun together, and share each other's pleasures.

We decided to get married when we were nineteen years of age. Although over 40 years have elapsed since our wedding, we can still remember the shock our announcement caused some of our relatives. Reactions ranged from mild protest to rage. In a few instances, there were long weeping sessions. We had known each other since childhood. Despite temperamental differences, the relationship had consistently been filled with fun and pleasure. We assumed that if we got married, we'd have a lot more fun and pleasure.

No one else saw it that way. We remember one evening

sitting around a kitchen table listening to an uncle, his finger wagging menacingly: "Don't you kids realized how crazy you're behaving? Marriage means responsibilities." "Marriage is fun," we countered.

He looked at us curiously. "That's how you see marriage?" He threw up his hands in despair. Our childish naivete obviously appalled him. "Your marriage will never last," he prophesied. "Someday you'll come crying to me. I'll be the first to tell you, 'I told you so.' Marriage," he said in a solemn tone, his words punctuated with pauses, "is a serious business not to be taken lightly and you think it's fun and games." It was clear that he thought it impossible to reason with blind youth. "Let them learn the hard way," he told others in the family who weren't able to block our decision.

We hoped that wedding gifts would include camping equipment, a case of tennis balls, tennis rackets, perhaps racing bicycles from an affluent cousin. Our list of what we wanted was held up to ridicule. We could persist in being innocent about the real world of marriage, but family and friends weren't going to participate in our myth.

The traditional gifts of pots, pans, toasters, a vacuum cleaner, dish towels, and a ledger to keep household accounts was not only depressing but, we felt, intended to shock us back to reality. They communicated the message: "This is what marriage is all about. Now settle down and grow up." Given this history, it is not at all surprising that, on our 25th anniversary, we indulged ourselves with purchases of ten-speed bicycles and on our fourtieth, the most expensive graphite tennis rackets we could afford and a case of tennis balls.

It would be misleading if we said that all these years have been a round of pleasure and fun. Like every couple,

Sharing Fun and Pleasure

there were times when we had to face harsh realities of everyday life. Places had to be found to live. One-room studios, fourth-floor walk-ups eventually had to give way to a purchase of a house and never-ending mortgage payments. Bank accounts had to be kept open and reasonably solvent. Baskets of laundry piled up. There were disaster days when the washing machine broke and the basement flooded. We have been confined indoors in raging snowstorms—trying desperately to amuse children sick with colds. We were and are not immune to problems. However, the critical question we always ask is, "To what degree are the mechanics of living, the ups and downs of life more important than the motivation that prompted our marriage?" It is a question all too easily forgotten or thrust aside when everyday problems seem a bit much.

We were certainly not unique in our motivation to get married for fun and pleasure. Without exception, couples happily married, and individuals separated or divorced gave precisely the same answer to the question, "What was the most important reason you decided to get married to your husband/wife?" The words may have varied. The messages were identical. "I married Eugene because he was fun to be with. I couldn't wait to get together on dates." "I married Sara because she was the first girl I felt comfortable with. We'd be together and every time was a good time."

Later, if the marriage dissolves, the couples will individually analyze the reasons and come up with all sorts of examples: she was child-like; I felt mature; he was too dependent and I felt like I was a second mother to him; he was monumentally egocentric and never realized I was an individual; or she closed down to anything new I'd suggest. This is only a sampling of post-marriage excuses for break-ups.

In fact, what these individuals are really saying is that the other person in the marriage is no longer part of the fun and pleasure of the relationship.

Why might couples have lost sight of the basic reason for marriage—to share fun and pleasure? We think the problem in our culture is that marriage has unfortunately taken on many of the characteristics of the business world. One of the favorite words is *work*. If a marriage is to be successful, couples must *work* at the process. Nonsense! Marriage is not a synonym for work. When these same two people were rushing out of offices at five o'clock premarriage and they met at a restaurant for dinner or went to a movie, they didn't think about working at having a good time. The aspects of a good time fell naturally into place. It wasn't a conscious effort. She didn't have to think, "Now I will laugh at his joke," nor did he say to himself, "Now I will take notes on what she has said so she will think I'm thoughtful." Couples don't date in the same spirit they bring to a business conference. Classifying marriage with business terminology and demanding that marriage use good corporation techniques for success is not only inappropriate but hurtful.

We don't for a moment deny the reality that the mechanics of living, responsibilities, endless details of day-to-day life are predictable, often boring, and necessary. But what has happened is that the contractual business aspects of so many marriages have grown out of proportion and taken precedence over the fun or pleasure aspects of the relationship.

In the course of our interviews, it became evident that one of the reasons marriages oftentimes become "better and better" as couples grow older is that husband and wife acquire the knack of focusing on what is significant.

Sharing Fun and Pleasure

The trivia or mechanics of life are put in their proper perspective.

Dorothy and John, the longest-married couple in our survey, have been together for over fifty years. They still walk hand in hand along a beach on a sunny weekend day, just as they have for all the years that have gone before. There was a time when the water's temperature didn't keep them from a swim. Now they only plunge in when the water and air are warm.

"She's fun," John told us. "She was fun when she was my Saturday night date—more fun now," he added with a smile. Dorothy agreed. Like every couple, they have had their share of worries, such as how to meet a mortgage payment when John lost his job and a second baby was on its way. There was a bad time when a daughter had scarlet fever. The list of their ups and downs could parallel the list of nearly every married couple.

"What we learned over the years," said Dorothy, "is to see what *counts* and what *has* to be done. They're different." Dorothy remembered when she first learned this lesson. "The kids were about 6 and 4. Joey, the 6-year-old, was a terror. I remember the day. Everything had gone wrong. Joey flooded the yard. I had told him not to turn on the garden hose. The hot water heater had a leak. You name it—it happened. I couldn't wait for John to come home. We were supposed to go to a bowling league party that evening. He opened the door and I told him 'no way' were we going to walk out on the mess. I have never seen him explode like he did. One word led to another and I wasn't going to give and he wasn't. He walked out that night. I was on the phone with my folks, my in-laws. Everyone felt terrible. His own mother told me, 'Just like John—fun first.' She agreed with me that it was terrible, his walking out like that with the hot water heater not working—to go bowling, no less. Everyone told me, 'John has to grow up. He has to be taught what comes first—hot water heaters come before bowling parties.'"

John said that he didn't tell Dorothy until much later that he hadn't gone bowling as she thought when he returned at dawn the next morning: "I spent a lot of time thinking. I was 32. Each day another list. I tell you, I was scared that night—scared of what was ahead of me for the rest of my life. No one worked harder than I did. I knew the hot water heater needed to be fixed, but there was nothing we could do about it that night anyhow. I told her when I got home that short of the house burning down, or something serious with the kids, when we were going to have a little fun, we were going to do it, or she could sit the rest of her life alone in the house with her lists."

The common thread running through the reports of all happy successful marriages was fun and pleasure. There is no blueprint or formula for what should be fun. For some it was sex; others talked about camping, hiking, dancing, sports. And what was especially intriguing was that the fun or pleasure many couples enjoyed was sometimes unrelated to money! Peter and Anne, who have been married for fifteen years, said they had the least amount of fun last year when they spent a lot of money on a vacation cruise. The constant dressing up and huge meals were too much for both of them. She cited this example in contrast to what the two of them found really idyllic. "Give me a summer evening after the kids are in bed, and Peter and I can go into the yard, have coffee, joke around with each other like we did when we were teenagers—maybe just gossiping or talking about whatever."

Sharing Fun and Pleasure

"Anything that breaks the routine is fun," said Kay. Married for eight years, Kay has two children. She is not working at the moment but plans on returning to work after the children go off to school. "I missed more than anything else not seeing Allan during the day. When I was working we used to meet sometimes for lunch. Last year I had had it. I realized we were losing each other."

Once a week, and sometimes more, depending on the weather, Kay tries to meet her husband for lunch. "The kids are in a play group four afternoons a week. I walk out of the house—dirty dishes and all—and I meet Allan. Fun for us is having lunch at McDonald's without two kids spilling tons of catsup over french fries. My girlfriends think I'm crazy," said Kay. "I know better. It's like an affair all over again for the two of us."

The one common link among unhappy, separated, or divorced couples was the absence of fun or shared pleasure. Mira, 31, told us: "Who has time for funning? We both have tight schedules." It was clear that Mira, like many others in unhappy or failed relationships, considered fun and play rather immature and for children. Adults don't play. Marriage is a serious business; you must be organized, systemized, and computerized.

We chatted with Mira and her husband Ron in their apartment. Two giant paper clips marked "His" and "Hers" were on a stand near the front door. A pencil dangled from a pad of paper. They were immensely proud of a system that was to "save" a marriage that had dissolved into a world of gripes. "We were both on the go," said Mira. "Nothing was done around the house. Neither of us could stand the cyclone of junk."

Ron told us Mira had become bitter because she felt he had become very male chauvinist, not carrying his share of their mutual responsibilities. "I ended up cleaning, doing the laundry, taking clothes to the cleaners. It never occurred to Ron to check if we had milk in the refrigerator." Ron said he wasn't indifferent, but he admitted forgetting his share of chores.

The lists were awesome. Ron is to clean the kitty litter box. Mira is to do the laundry. Ron is to shop on Saturdays while Mira goes to the hairdresser's. We scanned the week's lists. Nowhere did we note fun, pleasure, laugh a bit, enjoy each other! We asked them about this aspect of their relationship. "Of course, said Mira, "we socialize." Ron said, "We try to go out to dinner a couple of times a month to a really nice place."

"You know," said Mira, "If we followed your advice about fun and pleasure, nothing would get done. Do you realize what life would be like? I can see the laundry stacks now." It was rather hard for us to believe that the smiling, laughing people we saw in the array of wedding photos on the mantle—one with Ron holding Mira up in the air, her head tilted back, joy on her face—had gone through this ceremony just to settle down and check off lists!

What happens to the mechanics of life with the happily married couples? Is laundry undone? Do dishes pile up in the sink? Is the yard unmowed? This is far from the case. In our own life we know that when we have been having a healthy dose of fun and pleasure, who does what at what time doesn't seem to make all that much difference. Somehow dishes are put in a dishwasher and the checkbook gets balanced with far less argument than during those times when we have lost sight of why we got married in the first place!

Sue, a woman happily married for eighteen years, said she never thinks much about who does what. "When you get right down to it," she reflected, "I guess I do more inside the house than Steven. But when we're going somewhere we both want to go he'll do the dishes and empty garbage. I'll put away the lawn mower."

Since they both work now that the children are in school, we wondered how she felt about the division of labor. "I guess Steven and I don't think about it that way. We both know we're working. Steve is more serious than I am. I think it would worry him more if something wasn't done on time. There are times when I'll gripe, but then I tell myself I don't think Steve married me because I can fold a contour sheet without lumps—they're hard to fold—and I don't think I married him because he was the kind of man who remembers to rinse off the dishes before putting them in a dishwasher!"

With the unhappy, separated, or divorced couple, the absence of pleasure or fun was the principal reason for their marital dissatisfaction.

Rob, 37, an insurance executive, described the events leading up to the dissolution of his marriage: "I had known Jeanie [his former wife] since my first year in college. We met during freshman orientation. I can remember what attracted me to her. She seemed to be the only girl laughing, enjoying herself. The rest of us were scared. She came up to me. The first date was a walk along the campus. We each paid for our own ice cream. I think that image of her stays in my mind more than anything else—laughing and wanting a good time. We married after graduation. We ended up with a house, two kids, and a noose of schedules that got tighter and tighter. We were both working. Half the time we couldn't even get vacations together. About a year ago it started to gnaw at me. I didn't feel like going home after work. I knew I'd hear about a problem. The housekeeper was sick; my wife had to stay overtime. It was easy to go our separate ways. It got to the point where I felt I had better add sex to the schedule of our lives—11 to 11:15 on alternate Sundays before I mowed the yard and watched the kids so she could catch up on her sleep."

It is a fact that couples report they don't argue, worry about who is doing what, or focus on problems when they are having fun or sharing pleasure. However, it is true that when the pleasure or fun part of the relationship is absent, the couple concentrates on the serious business of marriage. They mistakenly assume that if they began working at the relationship they will insure against becoming another divorce statistic. Working at a marriage invariably consists of doing something about the mechanics of living. "I know things would be better in our marriage," said Marlene, "if Jimmy would only do the laundry once in a while. I'd feel a whole lot better if he helped." Jimmy's complaint was his wife permitting her family to make too many demands. "I can't see why we have to go over for Sunday breakfast and sit around with her parents. It's the one time of the week we have some free time. I would like to spend it alone without family."

Marlene and Jimmy couldn't be more wrong. Marlene may gain a moment of satisfaction when Jimmy does the laundry. But her contentment will only be very short-lived. We feel fairly confident that she will soon think up other chores which should be on his list. He, in turn, may gain some satisfaction when they refuse a Sunday invitation at the in-laws. Both of them are treating marriage as a matter of points. If you do that, I'll do this. They have completely lost sight of the reason they married which was to enjoy each other's company. Enjoyment is not a matter of gaining

Sharing Fun and Pleasure

points for tasks done. The model of the business world doesn't apply to marriage, where employees gain kudos for the amount of work they accomplish. The marriage may work efficiently but efficiency does not make a marriage work.

If couples persist in giving first priority to the mechanics of living, and relegate fun and pleasure to a back burner, they are insuring a future of discord.

No woman leaves a man nor does any man leave a woman with whom they are having a good time. After separation or divorce, it is a fact that when the individuals enter a new relationship their goal is to recapture the fun.

Evaluate the Sync of Your Relationship

This is a test to gauge the sync quality of your relationship. The test must be taken separately by you and your spouse or the significant other person in your life.

First each of you write down the numbers from 1 to 91 on separate sheets of paper.

Listed on pages 147–153 are pairs of phrases. Each of you read each pair. Pause and think about your current marriage or relationship. Select the one of the pair that means the most to you and write either A or B next to the appropriate number on your answer sheet.

We appreciate that you may feel that both phrases of a pair are important to you. However, we want you to make a decision between the two. You must say to yourself, "I have only one choice. Given this fact, which quality is more important to me?" Remember only ONE choice per pair is permitted.

For example: 1A fidelity of partner
              1B physical appearance

Although you may enjoy both, if you were permitted only one choice, which one would you choose? If fidelity is something you can't live without, write *1A*. On the other hand, if you can't live with someone who doesn't have a good physical appearance, write *1B*.

Sync Assessment Test

1. A. FINANCIAL SECURITY
   B. SEXUAL SATISFACTION
2. A. SEXUAL SATISFACTION
   B. RAISING CHILDREN
3. A. RELIGIOUS OR SPIRITUAL RELATIONSHIP
   B. HOW ROMANTIC RELATIONSHIP IS
4. A. WILLINGNESS TO SHARE RESPONSIBILITIES
   B. SEXUAL SATISFACTION
5. A. RAISING CHILDREN
   B. PSYCHOLOGICAL CLOSENESS
6. A. HAVING FUN TOGETHER
   B. SHARING SAME INTERESTS
7. A. COMPANIONSHIP
   B. PSYCHOLOGICAL CLOSENESS
8. A. PHYSICAL APPEARANCE
   B. RAISING CHILDREN
9. A. MUTUAL RESPECT
   B. HOW ROMANTIC RELATIONSHIP IS
10. A. FINANCIAL SECURITY
    B. COMPANIONSHIP
11. A. RELIGIOUS OR SPIRITUAL RELATIONSHIP
    B. COMPANIONSHIP

12. A. FIDELITY OF PARTNER
    B. WILLINGNESS TO SHARE RESPONSIBILITIES
13. A. MUTUAL RESPECT
    B. RAISING CHILDREN
14. A. RELIGIOUS OR SPIRITUAL RELATIONSHIP
    B. WILLINGNESS TO SHARE RESPONSIBILITIES
15. A. FIDELITY OF PARTNER
    B. MUTUAL RESPECT
16. A. WILLINGNESS TO SHARE RESPONSIBILITIES
    B. PHYSICAL APPEARANCE
17. A. MUTUAL RESPECT
    B. FINANCIAL SECURITY
18. A. PSYCHOLOGICAL CLOSENESS
    B. HAVING FUN TOGETHER
19. A. FINANCIAL SECURITY
    B. PSYCHOLOGICAL CLOSENESS
20. A. COMPANIONSHIP
    B. SOCIAL STATUS
21. A. HOW ROMANTIC RELATIONSHIP IS
    B. PSYCHOLOGICAL CLOSENESS
22. A. PHYSICAL APPEARANCE
    B. HAVING FUN TOGETHER
23. A. WILLINGNESS TO SHARE RESPONSIBILITIES
    B. COMPANIONSHIP
24. A. SOCIAL STATUS
    B. RELIGIOUS OR SPIRITUAL RELATIONSHIP
25. A. PHYSICAL APPEARANCE
    B. FIDELITY OF SPOUSE

26.	A. COMPANIONSHIP	B. FIDELITY OF SPOUSE
27.	A. MUTUAL RESPECT	B. SHARING SAME INTERESTS
28.	A. HOW ROMANTIC RELATIONSHIP IS	B. RAISING CHILDREN
29.	A. SHARING SAME INTERESTS	B. RELIGIOUS OR SPIRITUAL RELATIONSHIP
30.	A. FINANCIAL SECURITY	B. SHARING SAME INTERESTS
31.	A. PHYSICAL APPEARANCE	B. SEXUAL SATISFACTION
32.	A. RAISING CHILDREN	B. FINANCIAL SECURITY
33.	A. PHYSICAL APPEARANCE	B. SOCIAL STATUS
34.	A. SEXUAL SATISFACTION	B. SHARING SAME INTERESTS
35.	A. WILLINGNESS TO SHARE RESPONSIBILITIES	B. HOW ROMANTIC RELATIONSHIP IS
36.	A. SEXUAL SATISFACTION	B. SOCIAL STATUS
37.	A. FIDELITY OF PARTNER	B. RELIGIOUS OR SPIRITUAL RELATIONSHIP
38.	A. MUTUAL RESPECT	B. PHYSICAL APPEARANCE
39.	A. WILLINGNESS TO SHARE RESPONSIBILITIES	B. SHARING SAME INTERESTS

40. A. FINANCIAL SECURITY — B. SOCIAL STATUS
41. A. COMPANIONSHIP — B. HOW ROMANTIC RELATIONSHIP IS
42. A. SHARING SAME INTERESTS — B. PSYCHOLOGICAL CLOSENESS
43. A. HAVING FUN TOGETHER — B. RAISING CHILDREN
44. A. WILLINGNESS TO SHARE RESPONSIBILITIES — B. SOCIAL STATUS
45. A. HAVING FUN TOGETHER — B. RELIGIOUS OR SPIRITUAL RELATIONSHIP
46. A. MUTUAL RESPECT — B. COMPANIONSHIP
47. A. SHARE SAME INTERESTS — B. RAISING CHILDREN
48. A. PHYSICAL APPEARANCE — B. FINANCIAL SECURITY
49. A. FIDELITY OF PARTNER — b. SEXUAL SATISFACTION
50. A. HOW ROMANTIC RELATIONSHIP IS — B. SHARE SAME INTERESTS
51. A. WILLINGNESS TO SHARE RESPONSIBILITIES — B. MUTUAL RESPECT
52. A. RAISING CHILDREN — B. WILLINGNESS TO SHARE RESPONSIBILITIES

Sync Assessment Test

53. A. PHYSICAL APPEARANCE B. SHARING SAME INTERESTS
54. A. COMPANIONSHIP B. SEXUAL SATISFACTION
55. A. PSYCHOLOGICAL CLOSENESS B. WILLINGNESS TO SHARE RESPONSIBILITIES
56. A. SOCIAL STATUS B. FIDELITY OF PARTNER
57. A. HOW ROMANTIC RELATIONSHIP IS B. SOCIAL STATUS
58. A. HAVING FUN TOGETHER B. FINANCIAL SECURITY
59. A. SHARING SAME INTERESTS B. SOCIAL STATUS
60. A. RAISING CHILDREN B. RELIGIOUS OR SPIRITUAL RELATIONSHIP
61. A. RELIGIOUS OR SPIRITUAL RELATIONSHIP B. SEXUAL SATISFACTION
62. A. PSYCHOLOGICAL CLOSENESS B. RELIGIOUS OR SPIRITUAL RELATIONSHIP
63. A. HAVING FUN TOGETHER B. WILLINGNESS TO SHARE RESPONSIBILITIES
64. A. PHYSICAL APPEARANCE B. HOW ROMANTIC RELATIONSHIP IS
65. A. HAVING FUN TOGETHER B. MUTUAL RESPECT
66. A. FIDELITY OF PARTNER B. PSYCHOLOGICAL CLOSENESS

67. A. HAVING FUN TOGETHER | B. SEXUAL SATISFACTION
68. A. FINANCIAL SECURITY | B. HOW ROMANTIC RELATIONSHIP IS
69. A. HOW ROMANTIC RELATIONSHIP IS | B. FIDELITY OF PARTNER
70. A. COMPANIONSHIP | B. HAVING FUN TOGETHER
71. A. RAISING CHILDREN | B. COMPANIONSHIP
72. A. SOCIAL STATUS | B. PSYCHOLOGICAL CLOSENESS
73. A. PHYSICAL APPEARANCE | B. COMPANIONSHIP
74. A. PSYCHOLOGICAL CLOSENESS | B. MUTUAL RESPECT
75. A. SEXUAL SATISFACTION | B. HOW ROMANTIC RELATIONSHIP IS
76. A. PSYCHOLOGICAL CLOSENESS | B. PHYSICAL APPEARANCE
77. A. MUTUAL RESPECT | B. SHARING SAME INTERESTS
78. A. WILLINGNESS TO SHARE RESPONSIBILITIES | B. FINANCIAL SECURITY
79. A. SEXUAL SATISFACTION | B. PSYCHOLOGICAL CLOSENESS
80. A. HAVING FUN TOGETHER | B. HOW ROMANTIC RELATIONSHIP IS

81. A. RELIGIOUS OR SPIRITUAL RELATIONSHIP   B. MUTUAL RESPECT
82. A. SEXUAL SATISFACTION   B. RAISING CHILDREN
83. A. HAVING FUN TOGETHER   B. FIDELITY OF PARTNER
84. A. FIDELITY OF PARTNER   B. FINANCIAL SECURITY
85. A. SHARING SAME INTERESTS   B. FIDELITY OF PARTNER
86. A. PHYSICAL APPEARANCE   B. RELIGIOUS OR SPIRITUAL RELATIONSHIP
87. A. RAISING CHILDREN   B. FIDELITY OF SPOUSE
88. A. HAVING FUN TOGETHER   B. SOCIAL STATUS
89. A. FIDELITY OF PARTNER   B. COMPANIONSHIP
90. A. MUTUAL RESPECT   B. SOCIAL STATUS
91. A. RELIGIOUS OR SPIRITUAL RELATIONSHIP   B. FINANCIAL SECURITY

Scoring the Sync Assessment Test

The sync assessment test covers 14 categories. The aim of scoring is to determine the categories which show the highest agreement and those that show the greatest disagreement. Scoring is easy if you follow the instructions step-by-step.

1. Make up two scoring sheets exactly like the following sample scoring sheet. On one page you will score *Agreements;* on another page you will score *Disagreements*.

2. Place your answer sheet (1–91) and the other person's answer sheet (1–91) side by side so that you can compare the choices each of you made to the various items.

3. Consider the first item: A. FINANCIAL SECURITY VS. B. SEXUAL SATISFACTION. If both of you chose the same answer, *A.* or *B.*, put a tally mark after *each* of the categories on the agreement scoring sheet. Thus, for the first item, you would put a tally mark after *FINANCIAL SECURITY* and another tally mark after *SEXUAL SATISFACTION*. This will show you that you and the other person *agreed* on an item involving these two categories.

155

However if one of you chose *A.* and the other person chose *B.* for the first item, put a tally mark after each of the categories on the disagreement scoring sheet. This shows you that you and the other person *disagreed* on an item involving these two categories.

4. Continue in this way until you have recorded agreements and disagreements for all 91 items.

5. Count the number of agreements and the numbers of disagreements for each category. Using these numbers, you can then identify those categories upon which you and the other person *agreed the most* and the categories upon which you and the other person *disagreed the most.*

Sample Scoring Sheet

	Total
MUTUAL RESPECT _____	
FIDELITY OF PARTNER _____	
FINANCIAL SECURITY _____	
COMPANIONSHIP _____	
RAISING CHILDREN _____	
SEXUAL SATISFACTION _____	
SHARE SAME INTERESTS _____	
HAVING FUN TOGETHER _____	
HOW ROMANTIC RELATIONSHIP IS _____	
WILLINGNESS TO SHARE RESPONSIBILITIES	
RELIGIOUS OR SPIRITUAL RELATIONSHIP _	
SOCIAL STATUS _____	
PHYSICAL APPEARANCE _____	
PSYCHOLOGICAL CLOSENESS _____	

Interpreting Your Test Results

This test of the sync quality of your relationship is one you and your spouse or the significant other person in your life can interpret together. There are no right or wrong answers. Rather, the test is your own evaluation of the relative importance of qualities and characteristics of a relationship. It is not wrong nor right, for example, that, when you perhaps are forced to choose between *financial security* and *how romantic a relationship is* that you chose *romance*. And, of course, those of you who may have chosen *financial security* in preference to *how romantic a relationship is* were equally right insofar as your feelings are concerned.

The importance of interpreting the results lies in comparing your choices with the selections made by your spouse or that significant other person with whom you have an intimate relationship. Together you can identify areas where you are in sync, where your choices were the same. These areas will obviously be strong points, and you can build even further on these strengths. However,

Interpreting Your Test Results

it is equally important for the two of you to identify areas where you are out of sync. These are the potential sources for trouble. In those pairs where the two of you were consistently at opposite ends, you might stop and reevaluate your feelings and needs and the feelings and needs of the other person.

The differences are a signal that you are not in sync, that you do need to look at your priorities. In no way does this mean that we believe that either of you should do a turnabout, change your mind just for the sake of agreement. What we are suggesting is that you step back for a moment and consider the consequences of these differences. For example, if sexual satisfaction always takes a second place when pitted against financial security, social status, raising children, or any of the other many options this second place ranking should be a signal to you that you may be headed in the wrong direction, particularly if your spouse or significant other in your life always chooses this item over the other alternatives. The two of you can, without any difficulty, sit down together and go over the pairs of items and your respective choices. The differences as well as the similarities in the way you think and feel will gradually become clear. Recognition of your differences in attitudes and feelings is the all important first step without which action cannot be taken. And, on the other hand, appreciation of the similarities can provide you with a stimulus to continue to stay in sync throughout the decades as change occurs in your lives-the inevitable change that comes with the passing of years.

About the Authors

Drs. Lois and Joel Davitz have been married and working together *in sync* for over forty years. Joel Davitz, a graduate of the University of Illinois, received his PhD from Columbia University. A Ford Foundation fellow, faculty member at Yale University, he has been a Professor of Psychology at Teachers College, Columbia University for over thirty years.

Lois Leiderman Davitz, a graduate of the University of Michigan, received her masters and PhD from Columbia University. She was on the faculty of the University of Illinois, prior to becoming a research associate and faculty member at Teachers College, Columbia University for over twenty years.

The Davitz's have authored and co-authored fifteen books and have published extensively in the behavioral sciences in professional and national magazines.

For many years they have been involved in research on marriage, marital adjustment in The United States, Japan, and South America.